# BECOMING INVOLVED IN TEACHING

KENNETH T. HENSON
Associate Professor of Education
University of Miami

MARVIN A. HENRY
Professor of Education and
Director of Secondary Field Experiences
Indiana State University

# BECOMING INVOLVED IN TEACHING

Sycamore Press
Terre Haute, Indiana

**Cover Design and Illustrations by** STEVEN ROCKWELL

Library of Congress Number: 75-46377
International Standard Book Number: 0-916 768-01-5

3/7/77 Robert Tagler 9.85

TO:

Rex and Jo Ellen, who have recently been involved;
Randy and Kenny, whose involvement is yet to come.

We have heard you.

# ACKNOWLEDGMENTS

We wish to express our sincere gratitude to our many students who have permitted us to enter their classrooms and leave the doors open for other future teachers to see. We recognize their courage and trust that it will inspire others to give their best to the profession.

For those who gave their time and expertise to the reading and field testing of this project, we hope that our appreciation will be evidenced in the many changes in the text resulting from their suggestions. Dr. C. D. Farrar, University of New Orleans, and Dr. Cary Southall, Director of Field Experiences at the University of Missouri-Columbia, read portions of the manuscript in its initial stages and offered many valuable suggestions. We especially want to recognize the contribution of Dr. Patrick Daunt, Ball State University, who field tested much of the manuscript with his students in his exploratory field experiences class. We also wish to recognize Dr. Ronald Joekel and his colleagues at the University of Nebraska who read portions of the manuscript during the final stages of preparation.

Mr. Allen Sosdian, doctoral fellow at Indiana State University, screened the literature related to the topics in the book and was helpful in guiding us to many relevant resource materials.

Finally, to Ruth and Sharon, thanks for the many hours which you have surrendered so that this idea could become a reality.

KTH
MAH

## PREFACE

This book is designed for students who are exploring teaching at the secondary or middle school level in either the classroom or field environment. Its content and format most logically lend it to study in courses in Introduction to Teaching or Exploratory Field Experiences. However, the major topics which have been developed also seem to parallel those normally pursued in courses in Problems in Secondary Education and Issues and Trends. Instructors who want to stimulate methods classes or student teaching experiences and seminars may find that this book provides considerable grist for discussion and dialogue. In a more secondary way, professors of school administration, supervision, and counseling may find some of the content useful as a basis for understanding what the basic concerns of today's teachers seem to be.

Time and logistics preclude complete reliance upon participation as the sole process for becoming involved in so many dimensions of professional endeavor. Conflicts of schedules and travel difficulties are such realities that participation must be combined with realistic and practical study of the teaching process if a comprehensive picture of the schools is to be achieved. This book is an attempt to bridge the gap between the education classroom and the actual environment through the presentation of typical action situations with enough structure to confront the participant with several vital dimensions of teaching.

The content reflects the major concerns that were expressed by returning student teachers during a four-year period of time. Each case is an account of, or a composite of, a true experience or experiences. As the major concerns developed, chapters were formulated. As the chapters evolved, it became apparent that interest focused on four broad areas related to teaching: interaction with teachers; interaction with students in the classroom setting; involvement with students in the broader school context; and involvement with the community in a general way. Hence, the inductive nature of the content and organization of this publication represents those problems which seem to dominate the thinking of students who have returned from direct experiences in the schools. As these concerns are studied, the teaching candidate should become acquainted with the nature of the teacher's role and the problems and opportunities which he faces in working with young people--and that is one of the primary objectives of exploratory field experiences.

The sections of this book may be used in various ways. Through such processes as dialogue, role playing and video-taping, the predicaments and feelings of the teachers may be vicariously explored. Alternative plans of action may be pursued with other students, with the instructor, or even alone. Although courses of action may be implied, the participant must remember that the actual decision can only be made in the real environment where all factors are considered and where the individual making a decision must be responsible for his choice.

Each chapter begins with a pre-assessment which confronts the reader with a variety of beliefs. Ranging from the simple to the complex and the affective through the cognitive, they aid in the exploration of attitudes, feelings, and knowledge about the topic under consideration.

The case studies present true-to-life experiences which frequently challenge teachers. Each is designed to illustrate a problem situation and to encourage the reader to consider various techniques of resolving the situation. The analysis should continue with consideration of the basic factors, issues, and implications of the incidents as suggested by the section entitled, "Becoming Involved." This segment challenges the student to become competent in diagnosing the dimensions and complexities of a teaching problem and provides structure for value clarification through dialogue with peers and the instructor. The answers provided for the questions will serve as a basis of comparison, challenge, and reaction. This activity will help the participant become involved in professional decisions concerning teaching which inevitably face the educator.

The section entitled, "Field Exploration," is a unique way of relating concepts to actual practice. The suggestions are designed to have the participant test his decisions in the real situation as he enters into exploratory teaching. The experiences contained in this section of each chapter are intended to be used to the degree which reflects the needs and structure of each class. Some instructors will adapt the suggestions so that they more appropriately relate to their specific needs.

The section, "What the Experts Say," attempts to provide a type of "rudder" by presenting a combination of scientific data and scholarly opinion related to the problem under investigation. Although such a brief summary is not inclusive, it will provide some basis for speculation and comparison. Since today's student is eager to express his opinions, this section was placed after the student involvement sections. We believe that by first being permitted to express his own point of view the student will then be more receptive to the more scholarly findings. We believe that departure in style from traditional textbook orientation will enhance objectivity among its readers.

Each chapter concludes with a post-assessment, self-assessment, and references for further involvement. The post-assessment repeats the pre-assessment, and the reader is encouraged to compare his attitudes and views after he has been engaged in the consideration of cases presented in the chapter. The self-analysis encourages introspection which should help the learner clarify his views and feelings concerning his potential as a teacher. A chapter-end section entitled, "Further Involvement," presents some of the more lively and popular references which will help the student explore an idea in greater depth.

The content of this book is designed to be exploratory. The authors do not purport to provide answers to complicated questions. This writing is premised on the rationale that experience is the key to learning, and we have attempted to provide some typical problems along with enough structure to make them meaningful and worthy of further investigation. As students become involved with the guidance and assistance of the instructor, they should have more definite feelings about what teaching is like and about their potential to become members of the profession.

KTH
MAH

# CONTENTS

# INTRODUCTION TO STUDENTS

If you were to ask most young teachers how their teacher preparation programs could have been improved, the response in most cases would be to provide more actual contact with students in the schools. When asked why, they would submit that they would like to have known more of what a teacher's life is like. In all probability they would further state that they learned many basic skills of teaching through experience. In the final analysis, they will likely admit that they prefer activity to inactivity--involvement with students in an action situation in preference to the more docile nature of a college classroom where teaching is only described and discussed.

The book which you are about to read is written to help you capture a glimpse of the teacher's world. It is designed to help you confirm or reject your initial commitment to becoming a teacher, to apply college-derived theory to real situations, and ultimately to help you make an easier transition from the role of student to that of professional teacher.

Experience has demonstrated that learning is not necessarily accomplished through school contact. A teaching candidate must know what to look for, and he must spend his time in activities which have some structure. Otherwise, the situation may be rather meaningless as far as learning is concerned. A potential teacher should explore and seek to understand many different components of pedagogy before he makes his commitment to a career in education. As you participate in field experiences, you should investigate the following factors which constitute the basic components of the teaching profession:

*The school.* What really happens in a school? What is expected of teachers and students? What kinds of changes in students' lives result from their contacts with formal education? How is it different from a teacher's perspective than it was from your viewpoint when you were a student?

*Pupils.* How do students behave in a school climate? How do teachers react to them? How do they respond to teachers? What kinds of problems exist in teacher-pupil interaction? What feelings are involved in working with young people?

*Intellectual content.* What is being taught in the schools? Why does it seem to be a justifiable part of the curriculum? Do some subject areas seem different when viewed from the teacher's perspective? Do the challenges of a given subject area seem exciting enough for you to devote your career to it?

*Teaching skills.* What does it mean to teach? What skills are necessary to assure that students learn? What is the instructor's responsibility in structuring a learning environment?

*Decision-making.* A teacher is confronted with tremendous decisions. What kinds of judgments have to be made by professional educators? Can the dimensions of a problem be analyzed, alternatives considered, and solutions produced which seem effective? Do you like to make decisions? How do your decisions compare to the reactions of others?

*Teachers.* What kinds of people become teachers? Do they conduct themselves as you had perceived that they would? What is the teacher's routine like? Does it conform to your style? Do you think that you would like the life mode of a teacher? Can you cope with the school environment? Do you feel comfortable working with young people? Are you excited about the possibility of becoming a professional educator?

Your preparation at this time should heavily involve inquiry and exploration. This book is designed to help you do both by sharing problems which other teaching candidates have experienced and by providing some structure whereby you might more intelligently investigate the teacher's world. The material is presented in such a way that it leads from problem analysis to the formulation of generalizations about teaching. Problems are presented through case studies. After you perceive the problem, you may expand its dimensions through class discussion, activity in a school, studying information suggested in the book, or through other suggested readings. Once you have completed these steps, you should have information available which would cause you to make an intelligent appraisal of the factors involved in the case. Furthermore, you should have discovered something about yourself and about teaching in general.

This book is designed to help you analyze some of the facets of teaching. It does not provide pat answers which may seem to have no relevance in an actual teaching environment. Instead, it is designed to stimulate you to become involved in teaching through exploration and analysis in a genuine way. It should lead you to an awareness of the opportunities, demands, problems and skills of teaching. Ultimately, it should help you examine your own self in light of the type of teacher you can become.

# SECTION I

# BECOMING INVOLVED

# WITH TEACHERS

## Chapter One

# THE TEACHER'S CHANGING ROLE
# IN THE CLASSROOM

| | A G R E E | D I S A G R E E | U N D E C I D E D |
|---|---|---|---|

## PRE-ASSESSMENT
### How do you feel?

1. The traditional role of the classroom teacher is changing.

2. The new philosophy of open-concept education may cause teachers to be less respected.

3. The so-called changes in teacher role are merely contemporary terms for the same practices that have prevailed in the schools for years.

4. It is easier to teach "homogeneously" grouped students than those who are not grouped.

5. It is more demanding to teach in an open concept school than in a traditional situation.

### What do you think?

1. The teacher's changing role is involved more in the area of teaching technique than in curriculum decisions.

2. The open-concept school is basically different from traditional education.

3. The new programs in educational practice, such as open-concept education, will create more democratic behavior on the part of pupils and teachers.

4. The teacher is increasingly becoming a caretaker rather than an instructor.

5. Experimental scheduling is detrimental to pupil achievement and behavior.

3

## INTRODUCTION

The current decade is experiencing many educational developments: the open classroom, modular scheduling, experimental grouping, individualized instruction, and alternative schools. Furthermore, many people contend that the student and his attitude toward school seems to be changing.

The open classroom can create a different environment for both pupils and teachers. With the removal of walls, teachers can rearrange a learning environment in a matter of minutes. This new flexibility permits large group instruction, small group activity, and individual study simultaneously if the teacher desires. It also allows for more student movement.

The initiation of various scheduling patterns, such as the modular plan, provides further opportunity for innovative educational practices. As a result, we see some schools today which combine different kinds of scheduling in a new school design for the avowed purpose of serving students in a more democratic fashion.

Today's teaching candidate will need to know and adjust to a variety of innovations. This will involve the understanding of the basic assumptions of various programs and the opportunities and problems which are presented by each. He will find that there may be a considerable amount of criticism of practices, both from within and from outside of the profession. There will be cries for a "return to the basics," a plea for a less complicated type of instruction. Is it justified? Is the disenchantment (when it exists) caused by a reaction to innovative programs or a frustration caused by the times? How are the students responding to these differing types of instruction? What new demands are made upon the teacher?

The following cases introduce a variety of problem situations which seem to be related to revised concepts of educational process. The potential teacher should approach each situation with the questions: How would this affect me? Should I find myself in a similar situation, how could I best cope with it? What preparation do I need to teach in the newer types of schools?

## IN THE CLASSROOM
### Open School--Open Door

David Shelton arrived at Ventura School excited about learning to work in an open classroom with an interdisciplinary approach to curriculum. The daily routine started with a planning period which frequently drifted into talk about students. Some of the students' names became more familiar to him because they came up in the conversation regularly.

One day, while supervising a group at play, he watched one boy with particular interest. David noticed that the boy constantly changed the rules of the game in his favor. Suddenly, someone shouted at him, and he matched the name of Bob Funk with the conversation that dominated the planning meeting of Team B. As the days passed, David began to realize why Bob had never seemed a problem to him in the classroom--he rarely attended. It was difficult to keep class rolls in this school, and he was not completely aware of who was expected to be in class at a given time.

Now that David knew that Bob had belonged in his section, he decided that he would make a special effort to assist him in working out his problems. He began to have second thoughts, however, when he was unsuccessful in various attempts to help.

On one occasion, the teachers met to discuss student behavior and Bob was first on the agenda. The dean stated that the boy has an unfortunate home situation. Although economically secure, his family suffers in other ways. His father is a heavy drinker and his mother is emotionally incapable of handling the problem. He has two older brothers--one a freshman and one a senior. The younger of the two brothers is also considered to be disruptive. His older brother, whom Bob respects and views as a father figure, was recently arrested for possession of marijuana. Bob was visibly upset at this.

Now he knew about Bob and could explain his behavior. But, in a system which prides itself on being non-authoritarian and non-punitive, what could he do with him and others of the same temperament?

### Becoming Involved

1. What conditions seem to be different in this open-concept school?

2. Does the open classroom encourage misbehavior? If so, how?

3. Does a team approach help or hinder a teacher's success in attempting to modify the behavior of a problem student?

### Field Exploration

Ask your professor to arrange a visit to an open classroom. Observe closely to see if it is truly "open" in that students are independently working on projects and teachers actually approach students more democratically? How were teachers and students responding to the "Bob Funks"?

During your next class meeting perhaps you will be given time to discuss the two questions: Was it really open? Is it really working? After the discussion you may wish to write your own definition of "open classroom."

## Sunnyvale's Grouping Plan

The school administration of Sunnyvale Junior High School had decided to establish a modified method of grouping students. Instead of following the traditional pattern of heterogeneous grouping, they formed a number of "special" sections of seventh, eighth, and ninth-grade students, ranging from high to low ability. These pupils were intermixed for certain classes such as social studies, and then split into ability groups for classes in English and mathematics. This allowed for more individualized instruction, but the "chosen few" (as those in the low ability group were labeled) resented this kind of segregation and vented their hurt feelings in various ways. Their learning seemed to deteriorate instead of improve, and their entire attitude toward school seemed to be growing worse.

Mrs. Sue Bascomb was assigned to teach one of these special

groups. When she began her work with this class, she felt that she was not going to be accepted. It was very discouraging, but she was determined to succeed.

Paul Wible, a class member who formerly had progressed steadily, had suddenly lost interest. It seemed as if he had merely given up, especially in spelling. One Friday, when returning graded tests, Mrs. Bascomb asked Paul what had happened. He informed her that someone had taken his book and hidden it from him about three weeks ago. No one had volunteered to tell him where, and he had not asked for it.

Another incident involved a boy named Chuck, who was older than most of his fellow eighth-grade classmates and was soon to apply for a driver's license. He was simply scared that he would not be allowed to drive a car because he was in the "dumb" section at school. He also wondered if the insurance companies would consider this factor when he applied for auto insurance. As he talked with Mrs. Bascomb, he also mentioned that the other boys and girls had rejected him since he had been chosen for the "special" class.

Mrs. Bascomb felt that she should attempt to help these pupils. She soon found that she could get little support from other teachers. They rationalized that the students would soon adjust. Perhaps the whole predicament was the result of the new grouping plan, but she still had to cope with the individual problems which confronted her daily.

### Becoming Involved

1. Why did the work of some pupils decline in quality when they were grouped in the "special section"?
2. What are some advantages of ability grouping?
3. What are some disadvantages of ability grouping?
4. Could the advantages of grouping be realized without the students being aware of their status?

### Field Exploration

Ask several teachers for their opinions of ability grouping. What modifications in classroom procedures are made in classes which are considered to have learning problems?

## May She Never Know How Close She Came

Karen Banks inherited a group of restless students in an open-concept school. Her initial teaching attempts were generally unsuccessful, and she discovered that students seemed to constantly talk with each other and to generally ignore her. Was this the result of the more permissive approach of education?

After a painful week-end of decision-making, Karen came to the class Monday determined to provide a better structure. In order to make the class more interesting, she planned to initiate a series of games, spelling contests, and open discussions about a wide range of subjects. She would encourage creative writing and allow pupils to select topics that interested them. She would also try different seating arrangements, since the open space made this a very obvious alternative.

The second week seemed to be more encouraging as she implemented her plan. She felt that most of the students were working more intently, and some of the participants had even told her that they liked the class now.

In spite of her general success, though, she still had not reached Diane, one of the brightest girls in the class. Diane protested the new class procedures from the beginning and insinuated that she had been singled out as an example. She seemed to react negatively to every move which Mrs. Banks made. Through various means, Diane was encouraging the class to participate in a number of antics which almost forced Mrs. Banks to react in anger. May she never know how close she came.

The maneuver began when Diane started tapping her feet. Mrs. Banks adjusted to this distraction by sending several students (including Diane) to the chalkboard for a drill, while others pursued various individualized activities. While she was moving around the learning center, she observed that Diane was attempting to get a message to some of the students who were still seated.

Mrs. Banks was about to lose her objectivity. How could she handle this situation without causing Diane to become more belligerent? She thought that she might be able to cope with this problem if it were originating from a student who had learning difficulty, but she was exasperated in attempting to reach a bright

8

student who resented her efforts to manage the class. Perhaps she should forget the idea that the teacher's role is to help students discover a variety of ways to learn. Perhaps she should return to the traditional teacher role and become more autocratic. Her efforts to individualize and meet each student's needs had left her confused and discouraged.

### Becoming Involved

1. What initial concern caused Karen Banks to analyze the open-concept school format?

2. What moves did she make which indicated that she recognized that the role of the open-concept teacher was different?

3. Karen Banks has passed through an important growth stage in becoming a teacher. What is this stage?

### Field Exploration

Does one type of scheduling pattern reward or frustrate the gifted student? If possible, visit schools which operate on different plans and discuss this matter with the teachers. The answers may provide some interesting ideas to discuss.

## Some Wastebaskets Have Been Kicked In

It took Toni Bright a few weeks to become accustomed to the involved modular system at Willow School, but she soon became enthusiastic about its instructional possibilities. The flexible pattern allowed considerable opportunities for innovative teaching and the student freedom seemed to create a relaxed, informal atmosphere which she liked.

She was surprised to notice one January day that a faculty meeting had been called to discuss the effectiveness of the plan. The principal informed the group that the board of education was in the process of evaluating the new program, and he introduced the president, Mr. Watts.

Watts explained that it was the board's opinion that Willow School should return to a traditional system because, in his words, "This school looks terrible. There are signs of vandalism everywhere, and some wastebaskets have been kicked in." He then stated that he would listen to the expressions of the teachers.

Seven teachers testified to the credibility of the present system explaining that it was more demanding but that there was more time for creative teaching. It was pointed out that the school was located in a community where vandalism is high and that there might be even more trouble if the system encouraged alienation. The president dismissed the meeting without further comment.

Another faculty meeting was called on the following day. The principal explained that the board president had questioned whether some of the teachers had been sincere. He seemed to feel that the teachers had spoken in favor of the present system because of group pressure or intimidation instead of conviction. Toni was stunned at this interpretation.

The principal concluded by explaining that the entire board would soon visit to see the school in operation and then make a final decision. The impression that they received would have to be quite favorable or the system would be discontinued.

### Becoming Involved

1. How was Miss Bright's role different in this school?
2. How does modular scheduling provide student freedom?
3. What is wrong with the priorities of this school board?
4. What is the significance of the damaged wastebaskets?
5. Should a teacher ever defend a program which she does not believe to be worthwhile?

### Field Exploration

Ask your professor to arrange a visit to a school which has a modular program. Ask the teachers and students for their opinions of the modular plan. Are there more problems than exist in a traditional program? What are the advantages of such an arrangement?

### Who's Boss?

Miss Ramsey was assigned to teach at Ralph Wright Junior High School under the supervision of Mrs. Logue, the department head. Mrs. Logue explained that this school operates on a modular pattern which meant, among other things, that teachers had to be very thorough in filing reports. She explained that if a problem should occur the procedure was first to talk with the student and if this was not successful, submit a report to the guidance office so that a record of the incident would be on file.

One Friday morning, Miss Ramsey discovered that her purse was missing. After a thorough search of the school, it was found in Cindy Trone's locker. The principal said that there was no need to file a report with the guidance office since Cindy was to appear in juvenile court the following week and probably would be placed in custody because of some other violations.

However, the juvenile authorities chose to investigate Cindy's recent disciplinary profile at school before they decided her case. The guidance counselor reported that her school record showed no recent infractions. Since this was an encouraging report, she was permitted to remain in school.

Three days later, Mrs. Logue called a department meeting and placed the matter of discipline forms on the agenda. She clearly announced, "I don't care if you are in agreement with me or not, I expect you to follow my rules. All problems must be reported to the guidance office on the standard form." She glanced at Miss Ramsey and stated that because of neglect, Cindy Trone was back in school. Miss Ramsey knew that Mrs. Logue was aware of the fact that the principal had approved of her not submitting the form on this occasion. She felt that she was caught in the middle of conflicting instructions.

### Becoming Involved

1. How should a student teacher respond to her supervising teacher's instructions if they conflict with the principal's instructions?

2. Could this incident be attributed to the organizational difficulties presented by the unique scheduling pattern?

### Field Exploration

The case cited seems to imply that flexible scheduling causes

11

problems in regard to teacher responsibilities. As you talk with teachers, try to determine whether they are concerned about conflicting expectations from various school officials. Do they have more or less responsibility in making decisions about student behavior?

## Who Will Be Sacrificed?

Several years ago, a group of county educational and civic leaders began to formulate plans to develop a superior educational system through more efficient utilization of materials, time, and personnel. Three years after the plans were formulated, Avoca High School opened its doors in a middle-class community. In subsequent years it has subscribed to the objective of experimentation by utilizing learning activity packets, team teaching, and modular scheduling. Its advocates claim that this program has removed many of the physical and psychological barriers to learning which are encountered in the more traditional school programs. The three "R's" of the Avoca program are respect, reason, and responsibility.

The program was highly successful until federal laws were passed which made it impossible to exclude any students from attending. Thus, Avoca was faced with a new and different problem--how to assimilate students who come from diverse cultural backgrounds.

The influx of students from a different subculture seemed to present more confusion than had been anticipated. Teachers were admonished to remain with the plan of providing individualized, democratic learning situations, but their frustration level remained high. Teachers complained that they could not adequately work with students at all levels of ability. The quality of learning would have to be sacrificed for some students. Which group would it be?

### Becoming Involved

1. This experience seems to indicate that learning is not possible when two socioeconomic groups are simultaneously enrolled

12

in the same experimental school. Does this mean that new scheduling patterns favor one group at the expense of the other?

2. Are "respect, reason, and responsibility," possible only in experimental schools?

3. In what ways was Avoca's program innovative?

### Field Exploration

Ask your professor to arrange a meeting between your class and an official in the local education agency. Ask him/her to briefly inform you of all the current innovative programs in the local school system. Ask if particular types of programs seem to better encourage respect, reason, and responsibility.

## WHAT THE EXPERTS SAY

The emerging theory and research concerning open-concept, modular-scheduled schools seems to indicate that new relationships are developing between the teacher and his students. Although the adjustments may be somewhat uncomfortable for both, it seems that decided advantages are being identified through study of the schools in operation. The observer may be somewhat surprised at the student freedom, and the professional educator must come to realize that methods of student control which have been standard for so long may not be appropriate for the new system. The teacher's changed role seems to be that of advisor and consultant instead of director and authority.

In order to understand what is happening in the open schools, one needs to first be aware of the philosophy of open education. The open school is based on premises which point to a differing type of school and curriculum. The following six beliefs form the basis for the operation of many open schools:

1. The child is an active agent in his own learning. He causes things to happen by his own volition.
2. An individual may learn differently from all others. Therefore the school should help him find the way that he learns best.
3. The function of the school is to encourage exploration.

13

4. Teaching is more of a lateral interchange between two persons of nearly equal status. The teacher is a trained observer, diagnostician of individual needs, consultant, facilitator, etc.
5. The school should foster affective as well as cognitive growth.
6. The child has rights as well as obligations.[1]

Proponents of this system assume that learning takes place when the students participate actively in an informal, flexible environment. They assume that pupils are motivated when they see meaningful relationships between their school work and their goals. Since learning can also occur outside the walls of a schoolroom, students may be found in many different places and pursuing many different activities.[2]

The claims and assumptions of this new type of education are now beginning to be supported by research evidence. A ten-week study of an individualized non-graded program in English for the underachiever revealed that different teaching techniques did make a difference. When material geared to the abilities and interests of students was presented in an atmosphere which encouraged participation, students demonstrated improvement in language skills.[3]

Wilson and Langevin[4] compared pupils in two schools with open plan philosophies with a similar group from two traditional schools and found that students in the open plan schools had more positive attitudes toward school and themselves. Children were observed to pass up free time to work on projects, and it was submitted that they demonstrated self-discipline and maturity, and appeared to be absorbed in their activities. The schools

[1]Charles H. Rathbone, "The Open Classroom: Underlying Premises," *The Urban Review*, September, 1971, pp. 4-10.
[2]H. C. Sien, "The Open Classroom: A Critique," *High School Journal* 56: 134-41, December, 1972.
[3]Mercer Miller, "An Individualized, Non-graded Pilot Study in English for the Under-achiever" (ERIC Document 068 944).
[4]F. S. Wilson and R. Langevin, "Are Pupils in the Open Plan School Different?" *Journal of Educational Research* 66:3, November, 1972.

seemed to view problem behavior as being unfair to other people instead of labeling it as a discipline problem, and their corrective courses of action were more persuasive than coercive. Participants in the open school in this study felt that their permissive environment does not grant license to the students to do as they please.

Drayer and McLure[5] in a study of high school students asked the question, "Does the shift from a traditional schedule to a modular schedule have positive benefits in terms of student study habits and attitudes?" Comparisons of two matched high schools were made prior to and following the implementation of modular scheduling. Results indicated that there appears to be a strong connection between improvement in student study habits and attitudes and the school's schedule. Modular scheduling was found to have a positive impact, especially for upperclassmen.

Are students likely to disappear or become problems in an environment that permits unscheduled time? Although there must be some wasted time, it has been observed[6] that a sizeable number of students spend unscheduled time engaged in study activities despite opportunities for other activities. Students can (and do) act responsibly when allowed some time and place to get away.

The interest in open space, nongrading, heterogeneous grouping, and team teaching has prompted two educators[7] to publish a summary of research findings on the subject. Although conceding that there are no definite answers yet, the authors of the article speculate that these innovations have not detrimentally affected cognitive or affective outcomes. They speculate that nongraded programs can enhance academic achievement and foster positive attitudes among children. Overall, according to the authors, the research to date indicates that such innovations,

[5]Donald Drayer and John W. McLure, "A Comparison of Student Study Habits and Attitudes on Traditional and Modular Scheduling," *North Central Association Quarterly* 46:348-59, Winter, 1972.

[6]Everett W. Nicholson, "Student Use of Unscheduled Time," *National Association of Secondary Schools Bulletin* 57:105-111, April, 1973.

[7]Lyn S. Martin and Barbara N. Pavan, "Current Research on Open Space, Nongrading, Vertical Grouping, and Team Teaching," *Phi Delta Kappan* 57:5, January, 1976, pp. 310-315.

when properly interpreted and implemented, may be a step toward educational improvement and are, in any case, valid alternatives to the traditional mode of teaching.

One may then logically ask why the incidents described in this chapter seem to present problems for teachers, students, and other school personnel. New systems present problems and some teachers who have been accustomed to a more traditional school environment may find that conflicts such as those described are both possible and uncomfortable. It is almost a normal process to blame any school problem on the new scheduling system, as evidenced by the school board member who claimed that some wastebaskets had been kicked around. In a case study[8] of a school that implemented the new open-concept system, it was discovered that parents tended to place the blame upon the open-concept when there was a breakdown in discipline in the school. The conclusion was that problems of some type will develop regardless of how carefully any plans for innovation are laid. The prospective teacher should expect to see some problem behavior, but should work to establish a more normal situation rather than to blame the system.

A recent edition of a major publication contained an article similar to those in newspapers all across the country. The article, "Why We Must Return to the Basics," explained that twelfth graders are reading at the third grade level and tenth and eleventh graders cannot add, subtract, multiply, or divide. The implication is that this inadequacy is a result of the "new" teaching arrangements. But is this true? Not according to a team of educators at Indiana State University,[9] who explain that the plea for a return to the basics is only a smoke screen expressing a desire to return to an earlier and simpler society. Its emotion-laden attack blames practices such as open education for the fact that children are not accepting the values of their parents. In reality, according to the educators, students are merely reflecting the changes of the later 60's and early 70's. They conclude by implying that schools are

[8]George West, "Why Even the Best Prepared Voters Rebel at Educational Innovation," *American School Board Journal*, 160: 53-5, January, 1973.

[9]William Van Til, William E. Brownson, and Russell L. Hamm, "Back to Basics -- with a Difference," *Educational Leadership* 33: 8-13, October, 1975.

for students and should not be to indoctrinate students for a world that no longer exists.

In summary, it may be observed that the newer thinking about teaching stresses more individualization and student freedom. Teacher roles are different, and new patterns of teacher-student interaction may have to be developed. In spite of obvious problems, research is beginning to isolate certain characteristics which seem to be more adequately developed in an open school.

## DISCUSSION OF QUESTIONS
### Open School--Open Door

1. *What conditions seem to be different in this open-concept school?* There is joint planning, interdisciplinary approach to curriculum, and greater student mobility as evidenced by the difficulty in keeping class rolls.

2. *Does the open classroom encourage misbehavior? If so, how?* The open classroom encourages students to express themselves. However, misbehavior is possible in the most authoritative atmosphere. Most teachers seem to agree that for this reason teaching is more demanding in the open classroom because the teacher must tolerate more noise and more movement. Ideally, however, there should be fewer disruptions because the goals should be clearer and each student should be working on projects which interest him.

3. *Does a team approach help or hinder a teacher's success in attempting to modify the behavior of a problem student?* In theory, a team approach should provide greater input and a broader perspective for decision-making. However, a negative "set" can also develop in team situations unless the participants approach the situation from a positive point of view.

### Sunnyvale's Grouping Plan

1. *Why did the work of some pupils decline in quality when they were grouped in the "special section"?* Because they became discouraged when they were aware of their designation.

2. *What are some advantages of ability grouping?* The teacher is removed from the dilemma of trying to adjust the level of

sophistication and the pace of the lesson to challenge students with great differences in potential. The slow student is removed from the impossible task of competing with a student who has infinitely more ability. The bright student is not held back by the much slower students. Competition among students of similar ability can serve as a strong motivator, especially among highly capable groups.

3. *What are some disadvantages of ability grouping?* Students assigned to the slower groups are often discouraged. Parents and students often get exaggerated impressions about grouping which may discourage or even frighten students. Students in the advanced sections often become arrogant and lose all sense of humility; thus it may damage their social development.

4. *Could the advantages of grouping be realized without the students being aware of their status?* This has been tried in many schools. The result is usually that students know by the first class meeting that they have been grouped according to their ability and they know the level of the group to which they have been assigned.

### May She Never Know How Close She Came

1. *What initial concern caused Karen Banks to analyze the open concept school format?* It appeared to her that the more permissive environment made it more difficult for the teacher to establish attending behavior.

2. *What moves did she make which indicated that she recognized that the role of the open concept teacher was different?* Instead of being punitive, she attempted to enrich the class by using motivating devices and more democratic procedures.

3. *Karen Banks has passed through an important growth stage in becoming a teacher. What is this stage?* Karen learned to reflect on her classes and plan a systematic approach to attack her problems.

### Some Wastebaskets Have Been Kicked In

1. *How was Miss Bright's role different in this school?* She worked in a more relaxed atmosphere which allowed opportunities for creative teaching.

18

2. *How does modular scheduling provide student freedom?* Modular scheduling enables students to arrange for large blocks of time, affording them extended uninterrupted opportunities to focus their attention on topics which they enjoy.

3. *What is wrong with the priorities of this school board?* The comments suggest that the board members place neatness and orderliness above student achievement.

4. *What is the significance of the damaged wastebaskets?* The damage is symbolic of a breakdown in student respect for public property.

5. *Should a teacher ever defend a program which she does not believe to be worthwhile?* Since any teacher's first commitment should be to her students, her allegiance should be likewise. Therefore, a teacher should not defend a program which she does not believe worthwhile.

### Who's Boss?

1. *How should a student teacher respond to her supervising teacher's instructions if they conflict with the principal's instructions?* Since the prospective teacher is directly responsible to her supervising teacher, she should point out the conflict to the supervising teacher and ask her what she should do.

2. *Could this incident be attributed to the organizational difficulties presented by the unique scheduling pattern?* Not necessarily. The basic problem seems to be that of interpretation of guidelines rather than weakness of a system.

### Who Will Be Sacrificed?

1. *This experience seems to indicate that learning is not possible when two socioeconomic groups are simultaneously enrolled in the same experimental school. Does this mean that new scheduling patterns favor one group at the expense of the other?* No. There are examples of successful experimental schools from inner city to exclusive suburbs. The problem here seems to be that of establishing "reason, respect, and responsibility," in a school system which has had a sudden influx of new students.

2. *Are "respect, reason, and responsibility," possible only in experimental schools?* Such a philosophy may be more often ad-

vocated by such schools and may possibly be more evidenced. However, such factors may transcend organizational sequences and depend more upon the school's leadership or its individual teacher philosophies.

3. *In what ways was Avoca's program innovative?* It used team teaching, modular scheduling, and learning activity packets.

|  | A G R E E | D I S A G R E E | U N D E C I D E D |
|---|---|---|---|
| **POST-ASSESSMENT** | | | |

## How do you feel?

1. The traditional role of the classroom teacher is changing.   — — —

2. The new philosophy of open-concept education may cause teachers to be less respected.   — — —

3. The so-called changes in teacher role are merely contemporary terms for the same practices that have prevailed in the schools for years.   — — —

4. It is easier to teach homogeneously grouped students than those who are not grouped.   — — —

5. It is more demanding to teach in an open concept school than in a traditional situation.   — — —

## What do you think?

1. The teacher's changing role is involved more in the area of teaching technique than in curriculum decisions.   — — —

2. The open-concept school is basically different from traditional education.   — — —

3. The new programs in educational practice, such as open-concept education, will create more democratic behavior on the part of the pupils and teachers.   — — —

4. The teacher is increasingly becoming a caretaker rather than an instructor.   — — —

5. Experimental scheduling is detrimental to pupil achievement and behavior.   — — —

**SELF-ASSESSMENT:**

Now that you have completed the post-assessment, compare your pre- and post-assessment scores. Check those items where there is disagreement between responses.

Examine your reasons for changing your responses. When possible, cite the specific reason which had some influence on that change.

1. What do you know about the effect of new school curricular programs upon the teacher's changing role in the classroom?

2. What are your basic attitudes toward experimental learning situations?

3. What skills and attitudes are needed in order for a teacher to effectively cope with the demands of today's schools?

4. What do you know and believe about:

   a. grouping students according to ability?

   b. open-concept education?

## FURTHER INVOLVEMENT

ASSOCIATION OF TEACHER EDUCATORS, *Winds of Change: Teacher Education for the Open Area School*, The Association Bulletin 36, April, 1974, 47 pp.

Presents the state of the scene in teacher preparation for open area schools. Chapter titles range from experiments with open education, through in-class teacher training for open education, and concludes with open education in the college classroom.

CUNNINGHAM, DONALD C., "Observations On a Modular Schedule," *Clearing House* 48:2, pp. 113-116, Oct., 1973.

Considers the use of modular scheduling and its meaning for the student, his parents, and the school.

KUHNS, EILEEN, "The Modular Calendar: Catalyst for Change," *Educational Record* 55:1, 59-64, Winter, 1974.

Changing student expectations and life styles are prompting educators to develop innovative approaches to organizing time and curricula. Describes how and why the modular calendar works, as well as its future role in educational change.

NASCA, DONALD, "Open Education: Is It for You?" *Instructor* 83:2, October, 1973, pp. 92-8.

The article lists a series of questions to help teachers determine whether or not their attitudes are compatible with an open education program. It also gives plans to set up and maintain open education techniques in the classroom.

SALZ, ARTHUR E., "The Truly Open Classroom," *Phi Delta Kappan* 55:6, pp. 388-89, Feb., 1974.

Examines the curriculum as well as the open classroom and contends that if open education is to succeed, it is essential to move beyond the traditional curriculum. Note also the reaction in the following article.

SHERMAN, GENE, "A Student Teacher's Reflections on the Open Classroom," *Instructor*: 83:9, May, 1974, pp. 14-15.

A teacher looks back at his experiences as a student teacher learning to cope with the open classroom.

SUN, H. C. "The Open Classroom: A Critique," *The High School Journal*, December, 1972, pp. 134-141.

Presents a discussion of both the pros and cons of the open classroom. Identifies those qualities subscribed to by John Dewey which characterize contemporary classrooms.

UNRUH, GLEN S., and ALEXANDER, WILLIAM, *Innovations in Secondary Education*, Holt Rinehart, and Winston, Inc., 1974, 280 pp.

Interprets the role of the teacher and adds new concepts concerning competency-based programs. Discusses the concept of innovation along with student opportunities and responsibilities in a student-centered curriculum in the open classroom.

WENDEL, ROBERT, "The Teacher's Dilemma with the Open Classroom," *Education* 94:2, November-December, 1973, pp. 185-189.

This article identifies some teacher concerns with open, inquiry-oriented teaching and also attempts to offer some advice on how best to understand the rationale and the application of inquiry to teaching.

## Chapter Two

### TEACHER PROFESSIONALISM, RIGHTS, AND RESPONSIBILITIES

| | AGREE | DISAGREE | UNDECIDED |
|---|---|---|---|
| **PRE-ASSESSMENT** | | | |
| *How do you feel?* | | | |
| 1. The problems relating to teacher advocacy are having an increasing effect upon the educational climate in our schools. | — | — | — |
| 2. Teachers should be directly involved in governance of the school where they teach. | — | — | — |
| 3. The teacher's prime concern should be the welfare of his students. | — | — | — |
| 4. Teacher rights should be limited to privileges in curriculum affairs. | — | — | — |
| 5. Organization of the education profession should be similar to the organizational structure of trade unions and management in industry. | — | — | — |
| 6. Administrative rights must supersede teacher claims in the event of conflict or disagreement. | — | — | — |
| | | | |
| *What do you think?* | | | |
| 1. The typical beginning teacher is uncertain about the rights that he has. | — | — | — |
| 2. The increased emphasis upon teacher prerogatives is causing polarization between teachers and administrators. | — | — | — |
| 3. Schools will operate more effectively if teachers, administrators, and pupils all clearly understand their rights and responsibilities to each other. | — | — | — |
| 4. Teacher professionalism includes the teacher's power to determine his schedule, curriculum, and teaching conditions. | — | — | — |
| 5. The educational code of ethics is practiced at a very minimal level by teachers. | — | — | — |
| 6. Financial considerations rather than professional concerns are actually the basis for most educational decisions. | — | — | — |

24

## INTRODUCTION

Some of the liveliest discussions in education today focus on the topic of teacher professionalism. Today's teachers, supported by their professional organizations and by new laws and court decisions, probably exert more influence as a group than have any of their previous counterparts. This new power frequently seems to create a breach with administrative personnel. Since many areas of responsibility are not yet defined, today's teacher candidate may find himself entering a situation where both teachers and administrators may be endeavoring to influence him to accept a particular point of view.

The most visible source of change is the sphere of teacher-administrator relationships. Teachers find a new source of strength in collective action; yet they frequently feel somewhat abandoned by their principals and superintendents who appear to be less sensitive to their needs and problems. The administrators, on the other hand, often feel that they no longer have the support of the faculty and are sometimes frustrated in their leadership efforts. When communication fails, confrontation is possible. We see examples of administrators attempting to assert themselves more forcefully and teachers who are more adamantly defending their positions.

Teacher independence must also be accompanied by teacher professionalism. How professional are educators? Many critics of education point out that too many teachers fail to accept their responsibilities in this area as seriously as they should.

Should teachers be involved in the decisions that affect their pupils and the curriculum which they teach? How do teachers respond to administrators who make unilateral demands and who may use veiled threats to force teachers to accept their decisions? What responsibilities do they have when they observe other teachers performing in an unethical manner? These are some of the questions which are being discussed in the profession.

You may hear the comment in the schools that conditions among professionals are getting worse. They will cite the gap between teachers and administrators as well as the fact that today's students may be different from those of a few years ago. But is there reason for such pessimism? Are problems stumbling blocks or symptoms of growth? Changing, dynamic situations are nearly always accompanied by problems of various types. As you consider the incidents in this chapter and talk with school personnel in the field, strive to discover what changes seem to be emerging in today's educational scene and what the profession will be like when you enter it.

## IN THE CLASSROOM

### The Right to Read (As Long As It Is Cheap)

At the beginning, Marge Kantor was not really enthused about the new compensatory reading program when her principal discussed it with her. She relented, though, when she became convinced that the available federal funds should offer possibilities of improved instruction. It was not until later that she learned that the contract had already been completed and that the query to her was merely an artful way of informing her that it was going to be initiated next year irrespective of her feelings.

Marge found that the program did seem to be more effective than she had anticipated. Several students were showing growth for the first time and they seemed to be enjoying reading. The availability of equipment, numerous resource materials, and a teaching aide certainly contributed to the more productive learning situation. Marge was wondering why she had ever resisted the change.

There was no hint that the program was in jeopardy until the day that a terse written announcement from the principal stated that the experiment was to be discontinued. Marge questioned her and asked why a successful practice was to be suddenly terminated without any examination or discussion.

Mrs. Warren shifted in her seat and offered an explanation which hinted that administration was difficult and that it was causing problems. "You will have to admit," she said, "that it certainly seems to make the students more noisy." She paused for effect and then continued, "Also, the program is expensive and federal funds are being discontinued. It is too costly for us to provide such a program with our local revenue sources."

Marge countered, "But I thought that the whole intent of the grant was to provide seed money which would help us institute a new improved curriculum with the district eventually assuming the financial obligations. We still have some materials and resources which we can use. May I submit a comprehensive evaluation to the board along with a recommendation that this program be continued?"

Mrs. Warren closed her folder and stood at her desk, "I'm sorry, Miss Kantor. This is an administrative decision and it has already been made. We have to consider the sequence for the whole school whereas you are only involved with a small segment of it."

"But I was not even consulted," she weakly objected, "I did not know that I could be innovative only as long as outside funding was available. I thought I was looking for new and better ways of teaching children."

"Look at it this way," she said, "You have had two years of innovation. It is better than none. Now we have to live with the realities."

### Becoming Involved

1. In what ways did the principal show a lack of professionalism?

2. Should Miss Kantor appeal the principal's decision?

3. Are there other ways in which she could change this situation?

### Field Exploration

When you next visit a school, ask several teachers how they would support a highly effective program if it were being discontinued. Do they feel that decisions of this sort should be made by administrators? When you again converge in this class, share your findings.

## Hail to the Mardi Gras

The marching band was school as far as Whitaker Jackson was concerned. He was enthused about the band's possibilities now that he was in a new school with a larger group and better facilities. He proudly displayed the band at parades and athletic contests, and his group had gained admiration and respect for its ability and finesse. His ambition was to achieve national recognition, and the students were caught up in this spirit.

The big break came one November with an invitation to participate in one of the Mardi Gras parades. Whitaker was elated as he walked into the principal's office to share the news with Mr. Waite. After hearing the proposal, Mr. Waite thought that it should be carefully considered and he promised to discuss the idea with Mr. Cannon, the superintendent.

While the administration was considering the request, the inevitable leak developed and the students became giddy with anticipation. The band boosters club informally pledged support and volunteered to provide chaperones. Weeks droned on and the needed permission had not yet been received. Mr. Jackson remained confident that the request would be approved and instructed the public address announcer to introduce their final basketball half-time show as the "Mardi-Gras bound marching Tigers."

The crowd roared its pleasure, but the superintendent was outraged at this unauthorized disclosure. He challenged the principal immediately and Mr. Waite said that he had not given approval for the announcement. On the following Monday, the superintendent announced that the band would *not* go to the Mardi Gras under any circumstances because it would be in violation of accreditation regulations.

The band was crushed, and the booster club conducted an emergency meeting to demand an explanation. Mr. Jackson supported the procedure until Mr. Waite called him into his office and told him to placate the parents--or else! This was an order from Mr. Cannon, and we will all be in trouble if this thing goes any further. He pointed out that he had done a lot with the band and suggested that Whitaker would not want to ruin the possibilities for the future by upstaging Mr. Cannon again as he did at the game.

Jackson met with the band boosters and said that the idea had probably been unsound in the first place, that accreditation policies might be violated, and that he hoped the club would continue to support the band in its future activities. The president complained mildly, but thanked the members for attending and expressed the wish that they may be able to participate in such a national activity in the future. The parents were obviously in favor of the trip but perceived that they would be doing a disservice to the band director if they pursued the matter further.

### Becoming Involved

1. How was the superintendent at fault in his role concerning the Mardi Gras decision?

2. What error did Mr. Jackson make?

3. Do you believe Mr. Waite's order to Mr. Jackson not to challenge the superintendent's decision was sound?

### Field Exploration

Talk with a few teachers in order to determine how they secure permission for matters needing approval at higher levels. Ask them who they think should make decisions similar to the one needed in this study.

## The Boy Who Wasn't Worth the Bother

Betty Nelson felt that a teacher should be sympathetic and courteous to all pupils. Although she felt that she was generally successful in projecting a professional image to students, she found that she was having difficulty maintaining civility toward Randy Coxmire.

Her first encounter with the boy occurred during the first few days of the semester. She had just started to explain the nature of her English class when a tall, slouching boy rambled into the room. He handed her a crumpled wad of paper which had been a neat admission slip a few moments ago. After shuffling to the back

29

of the room, he greeted a few acquaintances and then dropped off to sleep.

Miss Nelson tried to motivate Randy but she was met by utterances of indifference and hostility. When she admonished him and said that he needed to pass the course in order to graduate, Randy laughed.

"I don't care. I am only around here now because I can get some money from a fund as long as I am in school. When that runs out, I won't be here any more."

Miss Nelson learned that Randy did receive funds from an estate as long as he was in school and unmarried. She further learned that his behavior and performance were similar in all of his classes. The counselors said that his parents were older and that he has been pampered at home. There was little use in making any moves to solicit their cooperation in helping Randy to improve.

A few days later, Miss Nelson received notice from the principal that a conference was planned to discuss Randy's future at the school. There were rumors that he would be permanently suspended unless there was some evidence presented to show that he was achieving. Miss Nelson had not completely abandoned her efforts to reach Randy, but she was beginning to wonder if he was really worth the bother.

### Becoming Involved

1. Does there seem to be a legitimate reason for dismissing Randy?

2. What should Miss Nelson do?

3. Do teachers have any obligation to students who appear defiant and hostile?

### Field Exploration

Ask a dean of students to anonymously describe the most difficult problem with which he is currently working. Find out whether the school has permanently dismissed a student on grounds of poor attitude and failure to achieve. It would also be interesting to see how teachers and administrators feel about the use of a threat of not graduating as a motivation technique.

## Do You Wish to Resign?

Mary Billinger, the wife of a professor at the local university, completed her teaching certificate after her children had established their own careers. She had majored in special education and was humane, compassionate, and enthused about working with special students.

Her first teaching experience was less than adequate according to her standards. The first comment which the dean of boys made was that she should send any students to him for a "whack" if they gave her any trouble. She assured him that she did not think that such means would be necessary.

She found that many of her fifteen students were boisterous, hostile, and insecure. There obviously had been little systematic instruction prior to her coming. Materials were few, and she even did not have a chalkboard in the room. Other teachers avoided her class as if it were quarantined. Her pupils were regarded suspiciously by much of the school population, it seemed.

Her first act was to request different equipment. Instead of chairs, she wanted tables so the students could work together. She asked for a chalkboard and several materials, but the principal indicated that nothing was available. Since she was not satisfied with this condition, she took her plight to the assistant superintendent without securing the principal's permission to do so. She found that he readily agreed to her requests and she soon received the materials and supplies which she had wanted.

The next step was to attempt to help her charges enhance their own self-images by being socially accepted at the school. She asked the principal to schedule some blocks of time for the students to associate with the other pupils in physical education and some of the other skill subjects.

"Mrs. Billinger, these students are special because they cannot cope with others," he said. "I can't permit classes to be disrupted by these problem pupils. That is why we have special education. You should know that."

Mrs. Billinger responded, "I also know that they must be able to live with normal people and that society must come to accept them. I think they should at least be permitted to attend convocation programs and eat at the same time in the cafeteria."

He coldly questioned her, "Are you going downtown with this one, too?"

She instantly responded, "I will do whatever I can for those students. They are human beings, you know!"

The school year continued on an agitated note between the two. The students seemed to like her and she felt that they were learning. Absences abated and one student even commented that it was so nice to come to school and know that he would not be paddled before the day was over.

At the conclusion of the school year, Mrs. Billinger conferred with the principal concerning her year-end evaluation. She was prepared for criticism, but found to her surprise that the evaluation was better than she had anticipated. All areas were favorably appraised except for cooperation with administrators.

She had just started to relax when the principal dropped the bombshell. "I have talked to the people in the district office and we have decided to transfer you to another school next year."

She was startled, "I know that we have had disagreements, but your evaluation indicates that my work is satisfactory. I have just barely initiated this program, and I want to stay here and continue with it. As long as I am employed in this system, I feel that I should have some right to determine my assignment."

He quickly asked, "Do you wish to resign?"

"No, but I am going to talk with my local teacher's representative concerning my rights as a teacher."

"I would not recommend that. You are not on tenure, you know."

She reacted to the threat, "That is correct, but it is too late to release me now, so I have a valid contract for one more year at least."

She walked out of the office leaving a principal looking at a favorable evaluation which he had just filed with the school administration.

### Becoming Involved

1. What were Mrs. Billinger's priorities?

2. What did Mrs. Billinger do which created cleavage with the principal?

3. What did the principal do which suggests that he considered the special education students beyond reach?

4. What fundamental questions are involved in this case?

### Field Exploration

Discuss the concept of "chain of command" with both an administrator and a teacher. Is it necessary? Is it better for all to have teachers go through channels? Are there any differences in the responses of the two individuals? What are the problems and frustrations in devising a plan that is best for all concerned?

## Getting Them All To Get A Few

In three weeks Neala, a conscientious, popular student, would graduate as the class valedictorian. A few days before school was to close, she was completing a research paper which required study in the library, the domain of Miss Hallett who had been the school's only librarian for the past fifteen years. She had definite ideas about student conduct in the library, and actively enforced a "no nonsense" code of behavior.

Long hours of work in the library did not appeal to many students, and several individuals started talking one day after lunch. Miss Hallett stated that if the students did not stop, she would reduce the citizenship grade of everyone present. Neala went to Miss Hallett and asked that she not decrease the grades of all the students because some, like herself, had not been talking. Miss Hallett said that if she reduced one grade she would lower them all. At the end of the period, she announced that all grades in citizenship would be reduced one letter. Neala's B+ in citizenship dropped to a C+.

There was a school policy that any student who had a B+ average, was exempted from final examinations. With a C+ in citizenship, Neala would be required to take finals for the first time in her four years in high school. She felt this was unfair.

33

She related the event to her parents and they suggested that she talk to the principal who was known to be understanding. The next day Neala arranged for an appointment.

### Becoming Involved

1. Why was Miss Hallett's decision unfair?

2. Which of the following is most important in the ethics of this decision?

> a. Neala was a good student.
>
> b. Neala was a well-behaved student.
>
> c. Neala was innocent.
>
> d. Neala was very near to graduating.
>
> e. The decision prevented Neala from being exempted from her finals.
>
> f. A good record was being blemished.

3. Should Miss Hallett, a professional teacher, have the right to take this action?

### Field Exploration

When you next visit a school, take a poll. At random, ask the teachers if and under what circumstances they have used mass punishment.

## Hair Today-Gone Tomorrow

Rex Hastings was a young, enthusiastic teacher who volunteered to sponsor the Key Club because he felt he had profited from that experience when he was in school. Mostly through his efforts, the club was considered to be the most active one in the school. Quality programs were presented and member participation included attendance at state and national meetings. Since the club's objective was service, the boys spent many hours in worthwhile school and community projects.

Rex adopted a philosophy of governance which permitted a degree of freedom in club affairs. He sometimes winked at some of their out-of-school initiation rites in spite of his awareness of school policy which prohibited such behavior. The students understood this and kept him informed about any "extracurricular" activities which might have some negative repercussions.

34

The problem began when a new club member appeared at school on Monday morning with part of his hair removed. The rumors soon reached the principal that Dan Kennedy had been initiated into the Key Club and that some substance which had been put on his hair had caused some of it to fall out.

Mr. Hastings was called to Mr. Scribner's office.

"Were you aware of this initiation?" the principal inquired.

Rex responded, "I was aware that they had planned to initiate the new group, but I did not know that they were going that far."

"Were you at the initiation?"

"No, I was not."

"You know, don't you, that sponsors are to be present at all club meetings either during school or after hours?"

"Yes, but I felt that something of this sort was not a formal meeting."

Mr. Scribner continued, "Then I am afraid that I must replace you as sponsor. There have been complaints and if students know that this kind of thing can happen, it will spread to other clubs."

Rex protested, "But I enjoy the club and want to continue working with it. I can assure you nothing like this will happen again. I like the boys and we get a lot done. I think our record shows that."

"I have already appointed Mr. Harmon as sponsor for the rest of the year."

"The boys will not react well to him," Rex said.

Mr. Scribner replied, "Then you make it your business to see that they do. If any disturbance results from this, you realize that your position here could be in jeopardy."

When the students heard that Mr. Hastings had been replaced, they immediately wanted to protest, but he quickly and firmly admonished them to forget their plans and to cooperate with Mr. Harmon. "Don't rock the boat or you will do all of us more harm than has already been done."

The students, out of respect, accepted his request. Now the club has quiet, orderly meetings and no one is going to the state and national conventions this year.

## Becoming Involved

1. What professional attitudes did Mr. Hastings have toward the Key Club?

2. What unprofessional behavior did Mr. Hastings display?

3. What unprofessional acts did the principal commit?

4. Did Mr. Hastings react to his dismissal as Key Club sponsor as you think he should? Why, or why not?

## Field Exploration

Club sponsorship can be a level of involvement with students which is professionally challenging and highly enjoyable. Talk to some club sponsors including, if possible, one in your subject area. Ask about the problems presented when pupil relationships become more informal. Also ask them what guidelines they use when they have to make decisions similar to the one regarding the initiation ceremony.

## WHAT THE EXPERTS SAY

Teachers are insisting that they have a right to be more involved in the decision-making process of the school. By what criteria should professional decisions be made? First, perhaps, we must understand what a profession is. The following statement may give you some frame of reference in considering how a teacher should react to educational problems:

*Professions are based upon a body of specialized knowledge, principles, and skills that laymen do not have.

*Professions place the welfare of society above the personal interests of members.

*Professions require that members follow a set of principles and values.

*Professions require a high degree of independence in making decisions with regard to clients and their problems.

*Professions control and protect members so that members may provide high quality service to clients without fear or favor.

*Professions are organized to improve the conditions under which members work and serve.[1]

[1] T. M. Stinnett, *Professional Problems of Teachers*, The Macmillan Company, New York, 1968, pp. 55-70.

Given this list of characteristics, one can gain some perspective on the actions that were taken in the cases described in this chapter. The experts mostly agree that teaching is becoming a profession, but that it must continue to improve.

The demand for more involvement receives considerable criticism, for teachers are accused of wanting welfare items for themselves, such as an increase in salary and more benefits. While they are interested in these items, there seems to be a definite trend for them to want more involvement in the area of curriculum. In other words, the attempt of Miss Kantor to continue with her program in spite of administrative decision could be a negotiable item as far as teachers are concerned. Unlike the unions, professional teachers are frequently seeking conditions which will help students, according to the experts.[2]

Although classroom educators are seeking and securing more rights, legal experts still point out that school officials have certain rights as well as responsibilities in the areas of evaluation and retention. The decisions concerning these areas may have been inappropriately treated in the case of Mary Billinger (Page 31), but what is really needed and wanted in these areas? Teachers are beginning to express their desires for more specific external evaluation. According to Schmuck,[3] "simply presenting information that displays clearly any discrepancy between a teacher's ideal and actual classroom performance does not, in itself, promote constructive change." The reason teachers fail to respond positively to external examiners is that such evaluations bring anxiety. Perhaps this can be alleviated somewhat if teachers consciously attempt to evaluate themselves in a realistic manner.

Do school systems have the legal right to dismiss teachers? Yes. Unless there is a statutory provision to the contrary, the power to employ presupposes the power of dismissal; however proceedings for the dismissal are frequently regulated by statutes.[4] Generally, teachers who have not achieved tenure can be dis-

---

[2]Shirley A. Jackson, *Shared Curriculum Decision Making*, A Position Paper, Illinois ASCD, Normal, IL, September, 1971.

[3]Richard A. Schmuck, *Self-Confrontation of Teachers*, Oregon School Study Council, Eugene, November, 1973, p. 23.

[4]Jerry Robbins, *Teacher Dismissal For Incompetence*, Governor's office of Education and Training, Jackson, MI, November, 1973, p. 43.

37

missed at the discretion of the school officials. Teachers on permanent contracts can also be dismissed, but the grounds are more specifically defined and the procedures for dismissal give more protection to the teacher.

How free are teachers to speak out about school matters? Marvin Pickering, a high school teacher in Illinois, objected to the way money was raised and spent in his school. He wrote a sarcastic letter to a local newspaper which led to his dismissal. Believing that his right to free speech had been violated, Pickering took his case to the U. S. Supreme Court. The Court ruled that critical comments by a teacher on matters of public concern that are substantially accurate are not grounds for dismissal.

The Court ruled that free and open debate is vital to informed decision-making by the electorate. Teachers are, as a class, the members of a community most likely to have informed and definite opinions as to how funds allocated to the operation of the schools should be spent. Accordingly, it is essential that they be able to speak out freely on such questions without fear of retaliatory dismissal.

In a similar case in 1969, two teachers from Alaska published an "open letter" to the local school board making allegations (some found to be false) about ten incidents concerning the superintendent. The writers charged that the incidents were "definitely detrimental to the morale of the teaching staff and the effectiveness of the local educational system." Among other things, the superintendent was accused of threatening "to get one-third of the faculty this year and half of the remainder the next year and bringing teachers and others into public disgrace and disrespect". As a result of the letters, both persons were dismissed.

The Alaska Court ruled that 1) those statements did concern their immediate superior, 2) the false statements did not concern matters of public record, and 3) the letter provoked intense public controversy, and the false accusations were made in reckless disregard of the truth. The court upheld the dismissal of the teachers.[5]

[5]David Schimmel, "To Speak Out Freely: Do Teachers Have the Right?" *Phi Delta Kappan*, December, 1972, Vol. 54:4, pp. 258-260.

In summary, it may be noted that the experts suggest that teachers and administrators consider professional responsibilities in actions and decisions. They also recognize that teachers have more rights and are moving more into positions where they share decisions about curriculum with administrative personnel. Teachers have a right to speak out without being intimidated, but they also have obligations to be truthful and ethical.

## DISCUSSION OF QUESTIONS

### The Right to Read (As Long As It Is Cheap)

1. *In what ways did the principal show a lack of professionalism?* She signed a contract for the program without consulting the teacher involved and then asked for her approval as though she valued her judgment. Then, after Marge had worked with the program for two years, it was abruptly terminated without consultation with the teacher.

2. *Should Miss Kantor appeal the principal's decision?* It would probably be a futile gesture unless she is able to produce additional supportive evidence along with reliable cost estimates. The principal made a significant point when she said that she had to consider the whole program.

3. *Are there other ways in which she could change this situation?* She might ask the parents to write letters of support to the principal expressing their desire to have the program continued, and she could attempt to seek curriculum revision to incorporate the new ideas.

### Hail to the Mardi Gras

1. *How was the superintendent at fault in his role concerning the Mardi Gras decision?* He failed to make a decision and thus was a party to creating frustration. It appears that he might have hoped that the problem would vanish if he ignored it.

2. *What error did Mr. Jackson make?* He exceeded his authority by announcing that the band was going to the Mardi Gras. This was unethical in that this was not his decision to make.

3. *Do you believe Mr. Waite's order to Mr. Jackson not to challenge the superintendent's decision was sound?* It may be sound to ask a teacher to comply with an administrative decision,

but in this case the teacher was threatened unless he helped to suppress any dissent. In a situation of this type, he may wish to secure intervention from representatives of his professional association.

### The Boy Who Wasn't Worth the Bother

1. *Does there seem to be a legitimate reason for dismissing Randy?* He did not seem to be progressing academically or socially. Some teachers would take the position that both the student and school would benefit if he were suspended.

2. *What should Miss Nelson do?* She should first decide whether Randy's presence in school would be more beneficial to him than it would hurt other students. Since, at the moment, he seems to not be making any noticeable achievement, it would be an injustice to have him remain in school for the sake of receiving money. Perhaps he would become a more willing student if he were convinced that he was experiencing academic and social success.

3. *Do teachers have any obligation to students who appear defiant and hostile?* There is nothing that indicates that teachers are supposed to teach only those who are charming and cooperative. Indeed, students such as Randy probably need understanding more than those who seem to be model students. Ethically, a teacher must be concerned about each of his pupils. He should be empathetic, courteous, and impartial in dealing with pupils. Miss Nelson has an obligation to Randy. She also has the right to assume that she can secure some support from the other personnel in the school.

### Do You Wish to Resign?

1. *What were Mrs. Billinger's priorities?* Mrs. Billinger was child oriented. She wanted equipment and curriculum changes necessary to provide the experiences which the special students needed to learn to adjust to others. She was also concerned with protecting her professional rights.

2. *What did Mrs. Billinger do which created cleavage with the principal?* She ignored line and staff organizational procedure by circumventing him in requesting supplies and equipment.

3. *What did the principal do which suggests that he considered the special education students beyond reach?* He failed to furnish the needed equipment and supplies and he insisted that the mentally retarded students should be completely separated from the other students.

4. *What fundamental questions are involved in this case?* One question concerns the nature of professional responsibility to students. Secondly, there is the issue of whether a teacher has the right to demand certain resources and curriculum procedures. A third fundamental question concerns whether a principal responds to and serves teachers or vice-versa.


## Getting Them All To Get A Few

1. *Why was Miss Hallett's decision unfair?* She refused to individualize her discipline procedure, and she punished students whose only guilt was to be located in the same area with students who were violating her demands.

2. *Which of the following is most important in the ethics of this decision?*
> a. *Neala was a good student.*
> b. *Neala was a well-behaved student.*
> c. *Neala was innocent.*
> d. *Neala was very near to graduating.*
> e. *The decision prevented Neala from being exempted from her finals.*
> f. *A good record was being blemished.*

Any form of mass punishment is undesirable because there is always the possibility of punishing someone who is innocent. Since Neala was innocent, she should not have been penalized.

3. *Should Miss Hallett, a professional teacher, have the right to take this action?* No. The teacher never escapes her responsibility to behave fairly toward students.

## Hair Today--Gone Tomorrow

1. *What professional attitudes did Mr. Hastings have toward the Key Club?* He enjoyed the club and it moved forward as was evidenced by his devoting much time to it and by the club's involvement in state and national meetings.

2. *What unprofessional behavior did Mr. Hastings display?* He sanctioned the breaking of a rule forbidding initiations.

3. *What unprofessional acts did the principal commit?* Mr. Scribner had already replaced Rex before their meeting to discuss the charges. A teacher should not be dismissed from any responsibility without his first having an opportunity to react to the accusation. He also demanded that the teacher see that the students did not protest the change.

4. *Did Mr. Hastings react to his dismissal as Key Club sponsor as you think he should? Why or why not?* Mr. Hastings had willingly and knowingly broken the school policy when he permitted the group to meet and hold the initation. He undoubtedly deserved some type of censure. However, he was placed in a position where he really had no option except to overreact and possibly be dismissed. This is a relative decision involving the conflict between the best interests of students and the desire to avoid dismissal.

**POST-ASSESSMENT**

|  | A G R E E | D I S A G R E E | U N D E C I D E D |
|---|---|---|---|

### How do you feel?

1. The problems relating to teacher advocacy are having an increasing effect upon the educational climate in our schools. — — —

2. Teachers should be directly involved in governance of the school where they teach. — — —

3. The teacher's prime concern should be the welfare of his students. — — —

4. Teacher rights should be limited to privileges in curriculum affairs. — — —

5. Organization of the education profession should be similar to the organizational structure of trade unions and management in industry. — — —

6. Administrative rights must supersede teacher claims in the event of conflict or disagreement. — — —

### What do you think?

1. The typical beginning teacher is uncertain about the rights that he has. — — —

2. The increased emphasis upon teacher prerogatives is causing polarization between teachers and administrators. — — —

3. Schools will operate more effectively if teachers, administrators, and pupils all clearly understand their rights and responsibilities to each other. — — —

4. Teacher professionalism includes the teacher's power to determine his schedule, curriculum, and teaching conditions. — — —

5. The educational code of ethics is practiced at a very minimal level by teachers. — — —

6. Financial considerations rather than professional concerns are actually the basis for most educational decisions. — — —

## SELF-ASSESSMENT

Now that you have completed the post-assessment, compare your pre- and post-assessment scores. Check those questions for which there is disagreement between the two scores. Examine your reasons for changing your responses. When possible, cite the specific reason which caused your change of opinion.

1. What changes in knowledge were experienced from the study of teacher professionalism, rights, and negotiations?

2. What changes in value orientation were experienced as a result of this study?

3. What are the most relevant criteria for determining the rights of pupils, teachers, and school administrators?

4. What do you know and believe about:

    a. who should ultimately determine what transpires in a school?

    b. the responsibilities of teachers?

    c. the obligation of administrators to teachers?

    d. professional decision-making?

## FURTHER INVOLVEMENT

BORGERS, SHERRY, *Professional Ethics for the Educator*, Houston, Texas, College of Education. ERIC No. ED 100 943.

A module designed to familiarize the learner with the National Education Association Code of Ethics. Teaching situations are presented enabling the learner to decide upon an action if he/she were the teacher in the situation.

CONROY, PAT, *The Water Is Wide*, Penguin Books.

An account of a first-year teacher who defies the school administration in order to provide relevant studies to black children. The book was made into a movie entitled "Conrack."

LIEBERMAN, MYRON, "Teacher Militancy," *The Teachers' Handbook*, Scott, Foresman, and Company, Glenview, IL, 1971, pp. 718-726.

A look at the nature of teacher militancy. Defines the term, explains its dimensions, and indicates some ways of coping.

NAGI, MOSTAFAH, and PUGH, MEREDITH D., "Status Inconsistency and Professional Militancy in the Teaching Profession," *Education and Urban Society* 5:4, pp. 385-404, Aug. 1973.

Investigates the attitudes and values among secondary school teachers choosing to join union organizations, hypothesizing that status inconsistency among the dimensions of prestige and income is an important motive for militant behavior among secondary teachers.

NATIONAL EDUCATION ASSOCIATION, *Code of Ethics of the Teaching Profession*, The Association, 1201 Sixteenth St., N.W., Washington, D.C.

Presents the ethical code of teacher behavior as defined by the NEA. Probably the most widely-accepted statement on teacher ethics.

STINNETT, T.M., DRUMMOND, WILLIAM H., and GARRY, ALICE W., *Introduction to Teaching*, Charles A. Jones Publishing Company, Worthington, OH, 1975, Chapter 7.

Discusses teaching as a profession. Includes a definition of a profession and discusses the conditions necessary for the education profession to advance.

## Chapter Three

## FACULTY RELATIONSHIPS

|  | A G R E E | D I S A G R E E | U N D E C I D E D |
|---|---|---|---|

### PRE-ASSESSMENT
*How do you feel?*

1. Most schools have harmonious faculties. — — —

2. The teaching profession is strengthened when men and women work together as equals. — — —

3. There is a pronounced pro-male sex role bias in our schools. — — —

4. Teachers who cannot get along with other teachers should be dismissed. — — —

5. Once a teacher makes a decision, he should stick by it even though it may have been a poor one, because admitting the error would lose the respect of his colleagues. — — —

*What do you think?*

1. Teachers who have interpersonal conflicts with their colleagues are usually inconsiderate and self-centered. — — —

2. A teacher who finds himself in constant conflict with other teachers is probably at fault. — — —

3. If a fellow teacher purposefully annoys you, you should inform him in a diplomatic way before the annoyance becomes a conflict. — — —

4. When a teaching candidate is assigned definite responsibilities, he should have every right and authority enjoyed by his supervising teacher. — — —

5. Teachers who have more interpersonal problems with fellow teachers also have difficulty making their lessons effective. — — —

## INTRODUCTION

The first section of this book focuses on the processes and problems of becoming involved with teachers because teaching is vitally affected by these professional contacts. Regardless of whether you are an observer, participant, teacher aide, or student teacher, the impact of scheduling patterns and teacher-administrative relationships will be felt. This chapter concentrates on a third dimension which is fundamental, not only in preservice education but also throughout a teaching career—the communication and roles demanded in working with other teachers.

Personal relationships among staff members are quite important to the morale of a school. Furthermore, they are often the determinants which indicate whether or not a teacher continues in his position. It has long been commonly reported that most people who lose their positions do not do so because of lack of ability to perform the job. Eighty-five percent are lost because of inability to get along with supervisors and peers. Hopefully, this figure is not as staggering in the teaching profession because care is taken to avoid employing teachers who do not get along well with others.

Not all interpersonal problems result from stubbornness or lack of cooperation on the part of any individual involved. Many difficulties result from circumstances which do not have clear-cut right and wrong responses, leaving the teacher unsure about how he should react to his fellow teachers, administrators, and other colleagues. Preservice candidates, for example, may frequently wonder how they should relate to a teacher who has been designated to supervise them.

Faculty relationships involve two dimensions. First, teachers must establish working arrangements with each other. How do colleagues respond to each other as equals? What are the unique problems which are presented when teachers have to work together? There are personal preferences also which must be examined in regard to professional concerns. The present times also alert us to the fact that the possibility of sex role conflicts are quite real. The roles of both men and women in the schools may possibly be redefined within the next few years. Although the proportion of men serving as principals has increased at the expense of women in recent years, the situation may change as a result of the new equality laws. This move may be supported by a 1975 Gallup Poll[1] which reported that 52 percent of the national totals indicated that it makes no difference whether a principal is a man or a woman.

Preservice teachers and inservice teachers must also be aware of the fact that they need to work harmoniously with supervisors. This is more clearly defined in preservice activities, but teachers, too, must know how to respond to supervisors in a constructive way. The roles of each may need to be examined and understood in order for the teacher to thoroughly understand how maximum benefit can be achieved from such contacts.

The following experiences reflect some of the difficult positions in which teachers often find themselves. Perhaps as each is read and contemplated, it will provide insight into some effective approaches to reacting to dilemmas. If teachers are to fulfill their overall objective--that of providing the best possible education for students--they can do so only through working cooperatively with administrators, supervisors, fellow teachers, and other colleagues.

## IN THE CLASSROOM
### Choose Your Side and Stand Your Ground

The two foreign language teachers at Newport High are highly competent in their fields. Mrs. Teal received her degrees from a well-known university and has received several grants to work toward a doctorate. She has had several years of teaching experience and is well-liked and respected by her students. Mrs. Newley, the department chairperson, has an equivalent educational background with more extensive experience abroad, but her only previous teaching experience was for two years in an elementary school for underprivileged children.

[1] George Gallup, "Seventh Annual Gallup Poll of Public Attitudes Toward Education," *Phi Delta Kappan* 57:4, December, 1975.

Competency does not always lead to compatibility, though. Mrs. Newley is very interested in the student-oriented approach and believes in permitting the students to proceed at their own rates. Mrs. Teal, on the other hand, prefers to remain with the conventional style with some embellishment of resource materials. Her students scored well above average on the city-wide French examination. The conflict, which was philosophical at first, has enlarged into a situation where petty disagreements erupt, and open confrontations have developed over a few substantive matters. Mrs. Teal is quick to point out that she has few management problems and implies that Mrs. Newley's classes are shamefully disorganized.

The climax in the conflict developed after Mrs. Newley completed her required observation of Mrs. Teal's class. Instead of using the standard form provided for department chairpersons, she composed her own. The final report stated that Mrs. Teal's qualifications were good and her rapport with the students was excellent. However, she felt that Mrs. Teal's methods were somewhat inefficient, and her command of the language was deficient. Mrs. Teal received a copy of the evaluation and was upset by its content. She wrote a rebuttal stating that she would resign unless she was relieved from the suppression and pressure from the department chairperson.

The situation involves not only a difference in methodology but also a very real personal conflict between two well-qualified teachers. Furthermore, the discord cannot be isolated because it involves morale within the department as well as the question of how teaching is actually analyzed and evaluated in this school.

### Becoming Involved

1. What seems to have caused the conflict?

2. Can we say that Mrs. Newley's teaching style was better than Mrs. Teal's?

3. Why must the present situation not be allowed?

### Field Exploration

Talk with department chairpersons or supervisors. What do they consider to be the logical responsibility in observing and evaluating other teachers or teacher candidates? How are conflicts prevented when there are obvious philosophical differences?

### There is No Art in Envy

Mrs. Bryce and Mrs. Creighton were to teach art in adjacent rooms in the new consolidated high school. Although they had known each other when they taught in separate schools before the new building was constructed, they really had not previously worked together. Now they would be sharing some of the same facilities.

Mrs. Bryce is an extremely energetic person who constantly strives to become a more competent art teacher. She is considered to be one of the best teachers in the state and also has some recognition as a professional artist. Mrs. Creighton has taught in several communities since her husband, a sales manager, has relocated several times with his firm. She is affable, but due to the fact that she has responsibilities for five young children at home, she has little time for the professional aspect of the art teacher's life.

Shortly after school had started, Mrs. Bryce noticed some art compositions on display which had been created by Mrs. Creighton's students. It seemed to her that the work was very elementary for secondary students. A few days later, she passed through Mrs. Creighton's room and observed that she was permitting students to use the printing press incorrectly. Feeling that some damage might result, she proceeded to demonstrate to the students how the press was to be operated. Mrs. Creighton responded by informing her in the presence of the entire class that her students knew how to set up the press and that neither she nor they needed any outside help. Mrs. Bryce left the room without any rebuttal, but she was surprised because Mrs. Creighton had been unable to identify this new piece of equipment when it had arrived recently.

The next incident occurred when Mrs. Creighton burst into Mrs. Bryce's class and accused her of using some materials that belonged to one of her students. Mrs. Bryce explained that it was a mistake and she would replace the items. When her colleague

50

continued to complain, she was finally forced to turn away to prevent further argument in the presence of her pupils.

The two teachers met later that day and agreed that if there were any more differences, they should be discussed in private; not in the presence of students. The truce was an uneasy one, though, as conflicts continued to occur. By second semester, they only communicated out of necessity and the students were quite aware of the friction. At the end of the school year, Mrs. Bryce contacted the principal and explained the situation as she perceived it. The principal had already heard about the problem from Mrs. Creighton and had concluded that the basic problem was that she envied Mrs. Bryce and was jealous of her ability and of her student rapport. The conflict was too serious to ignore; both the teachers and the students were affected.

### Becoming Involved

1. What was the one unprofessional behavior which was seen more than once in the relationship of these two teachers?

2. Mrs. Creighton must not receive all of the blame since it was an action of Mrs. Bryce which initiated the entire development. What was that and how could it have been avoided?

### Field Exploration

Observe teachers who work together in the same subject. Do they convey any evidence of tension through their conversations or body language? What are these symptoms? Talk with teachers who obviously disagree with the style of their counterparts but manage to respect and work with them.

### Encounter in the Lounge

The conflict between the experienced and the beginner, the liberal and the conservative, and male and female seems to have its forum in the lounge at East High School. Today, it is women's rights day, and it began innocently enough when a few teachers were discussing the impending retirement of the present principal. Mary Francis, who had devoted her career to teaching at East High School, commented that she would like to see a woman principal at the school before she retires.

51

John Kester immediately intervened with the observation that there is no female who can handle the problems at this school. His comment prompted a barrage of challenges from the several women in the room. This was a sexist statement, they said, and he should withdraw it.

"Never," said John, as he warmed up to his **defense**. "In the first place, an administrator should be a permanent appointment, and women have a record of being more temporary. In the second place, men are better prepared to make the hard decisions that administrators have to make. Finally, a woman would never be able to establish the kind of control that is necessary in this school."

The women were unimpressed by his arguments. Jodi McNaughton was quick to point out that women establish careers in education as well as men, and cited Mary Francis as an example. She continued to defend the woman's point of view by reminding him that women are not a "mob of mobile maidens meditating matrimony." Indeed, they are more professional, innovative, and **conscientious than most men on this faculty.**

Before John could respond, Lynn Hughes cited a bit of research which indicated that women were not only as effective as men in leadership positions; they were found to be more sensitive to problems and more receptive to change. Indeed, control in a school should not be determined by force but by reason, and women probably can do that better than men.

Finally, John got in a few more licks. "The men in this building have to do more work around here because women either cannot or will not assume as great a work load." He stared at them and then challenged them to control his seventh-hour study hall. And what about all of those "family obligations" after school which tend to exclude them from evening responsibilities? "If you want to be paid like a man, work like a man," he fumed.

A chorus of feminine voices chimed in with, "We do more than our share of the work around here. It is you men who insist on all those evening activities by your enthusiasm for athletics."

He appeared not to have heard them, "One more thing," he said," you don't have to support a family on one salary. Teaching is just a comfortable second income for you. Try to make it alone on a teacher's salary, and you will see why men are looking for positions which help them meet today's financial demands."

The bell sounded, and a group of agitated teachers filed out. A new throng entered and began talking about the fact that older teachers are no longer in touch with the realities of teaching. Presently, the noise level in the room began to rise again.

### Becoming Involved

1. What assumptions are made by Mr. Kester in regard to sex roles within the school?

2. What valid point has been made by the women?

3. What are some of the underlying issues that confront men and women in regard to faculty relations?

### Field Exploration

The faculty lounge is an interesting place to visit. Preservice teachers are somewhat confused, but always interested in what happens there. Spend an hour or two occasionally as a visitor and listen to the conversation. What are the points of issue? What conclusions can you draw about faculty relations by listening to their informal talk? Do you see any evidence of male-female conflicts in the school? Do men and women tend to segregate themselves for conversation?

## A Matter of Communication

Elizabeth Carter knew that she would be supervised by Harrison Hunt, an experienced teacher who was proud of his reputation. She did not know that he had difficulty in communicating instructions until she became involved in some exchanges of media equipment.

The first incident occurred when Mrs. Miller, who taught in the same wing of the school, asked to use the filmstrip projector during the fourth hour. Since Ms. Carter planned to use it only the third hour, she agreed without consultation. When Mr. Hunt later entered the room and found that the projector was missing, he specifically indicated that no equipment was to be taken from *his* room. Although she was somewhat puzzled by this stern demand, she apologized and indicated that she was not aware that she was violating operating procedure.

A few days later, another teacher, Henry Smith, asked to use the tape recorder that was in the room. When he indicated that Mr. Hunt had approved provided she were not using it, she readily consented. She was happy to cooperate since Mr. Smith had been very helpful to her on occasion.

At lunch, Ms. Carter realized that Mr. Hunt was irritated about something. Finally he abruptly confronted her with the fact that she was again lending materials without his authorization. When she indicated that Mr. Smith had assured her that approval had been granted to take the recorder, Mr. Hall flushed and replied, "I did *not* give my permission for *anyone* to take equipment from my room and you do not have the authority to let anyone remove anything. Do you understand?"

Ms. Carter nodded and changed the subject. Later that day, she spoke with Mr. Smith about the incident. He assured her that Mr. Hunt had indeed given his permission to use the equipment and that she should not be blamed in any way.

Now she was concerned. What was causing the confusion? How could she get involved with fundamental problems if she could not communicate with her supervisor in such simple matters as lending media? To whom could she turn? What would happen to her experience if so much energy were expended in incidents such as these instead of a more comprehensive analysis of teaching style?

### Becoming Involved

1. How can you explain (not justify) Mr. Hunt's feelings about the equipment?

2. Did Ms. Carter act unprofessionally in lending the equipment?

3. Suggest one way in which participants or teachers may be able to communicate with teachers or supervisors whose directions are difficult to comprehend.

### Field Exploration

Most schools which accept student teachers or student participants usually have several preservice candidates in a building at any one time. Ask them if they have experienced any difficulties in communicating with their supervisors. How do they cope with unexpected demands or seemingly inconsistent behavior? Have they devised any systems which they have found useful in dealing with unwarranted criticism?

### The Grade Is Not the Same

At the beginning of Kenny Lloyd's student teaching experience, he assumed that he would be responsible for assigning the grades to the students whom he taught. He decided that each grade would be determined by such factors as daily attendance and skill development as well as his subjective evaluation of individual student performance.

Although Kenny informed each student of his appraisal in a personal conference, his supervising teacher recorded the grades on the students' cards. He was surprised to learn when cards were distributed that three students had not received the grades which they had been told they had earned. When they approached him for an explanation, he indicated that there had been a mistake and that he would check into the matter. He asked the pupils to see him again before the end of the school day.

When he went to his supervisor's office to discuss the problem, he was surprised to learn that the only explanation was that the students could not have improved their skill level enough to earn the grade which was reported. The supervisor argued that the students who had their grades changed had poor attendance records. She was not impressed when Kenny indicated he had already taken that into consideration.

In spite of his efforts, Kenny could not convince his supervisor to modify her stand and he felt that he really was in no position to press his point since it might reflect on his evaluation. He felt that his supervisor had not shown fairness because she had not supported his decision. He tried to understand the complexities but he was still nagged by the disappointment of the persons whose grades were changed.

He endured the day, trying to decide how he would inform

the students that their grades had been changed. The final bell rang, and the trio came down the hall toward him. As they approached, he became more uncomfortable because he still had been unable to formulate a successful explanation which he thought the students would accept.

### Becoming Involved

1. State one conclusion that can be drawn from the conflict that resulted in this case.

2. Who should have the authority to make the final decision?

3. How can such incidents be prevented in the future?

### Field Exploration

Arrange for several former student teachers or interns to visit your classes. (Ideally, they should have just completed their assignment and now just returned to campus.) Ask them if they ever felt that the supervisor had changed operating procedures and made the situation uncomfortable for the participant.

What are the principles that will prevent a situation similar to this one from occurring? Engage in a conversation with a student teacher and his supervising teacher when you are participating in a school. Ask them how they have established communication procedures so that misunderstandings are prevented.

## WHAT THE EXPERTS SAY

Faculty relations, whether they be peer relationships or supervisor-subordinate relationships, involve the necessity of effectively working together. What kind of situation is needed for teachers to work compatibly? George Homans[2] says that the members of a group influence each other until group behavior reaches a state of practical equilibrium. Some prefer his simpler statement that individuals work best together when each party perceives the

[2]George Homans, *Conformity, Social Behavior: Its Elementary Forms*, Harcourt-Brace, New York, 1961, pp. 112-129.

other as an equal. According to this principle, we can expect better faculty relationships when teachers, supervisors, and preservice candidates regard each other as equals rather than as superiors or subordinates.

The faculty lounge is an interesting phenomena in education. Student teachers are often surprised and amused by the behavior and comments of teachers. Is the incident described in this chapter typical? Perhaps in an exaggerated way it reflects a common concern in education today, but the dynamics of the teachers lounge may be worth noting. According to Dr. William Hinckley,[3] in the teachers lounge teacher symptoms include expressions of a negative attitude toward students, parents, the school building, the principal, the superintendent, and possibly the world in general. He further states that it does little to solve problems and is perpetuating and ultimately distractive to the school and to the student.

The discussion in the lounge concerning the role of female teachers in schools points to the problem of sexism in the schools. What is happening in this area? A recent issue of the highly-respected *Journal of Teacher Education*[4] focused on the concept of molding the nonsexist teacher. Stressing that the re-evaluation of sex roles is extending into the schools as well as other parts of society, it claims that schools are not meeting the needs of both sexes for either teachers or students.

Although research and opinion seem to indicate that women are capable and effective in leadership roles, a research study reported in the *Journal of Teacher Education*[5] points out that men who are teaching candidates are more likely to anticipate pursuing the doctorate and assuming leadership positions in administration than women who are teaching candidates.

The case studies involving the lending of equipment and the issuing of grades indicate communication problems between teaching candidates and supervisor, but they may also have the implication that the candidates would like to make some changes. According to one expert, much of the negativism which new

[3]W. L. Hinckley, "Boiler Room Syndrome," *School and Community* 60:23, March, 1974.

[4]Joel Burdin, Editor, *Journal of Teacher Education* 26:4, Winter, 1975.

[5]Ibid, pp.323-4.

teachers receive from more experienced colleagues results from the new teachers' desires to make changes. Robert Geiser[6] lists some of the more common teacher rebuttals:

"We tried that once and it did not work."

"But we have always done it this way."

"The students and their parents will be upset if you change it now."

"Good idea, but it is against regulations."

Geiser concludes that the new teacher can improve his relationships with his colleagues by accepting the fact that he cannot bring substantial change to the program rapidly. Furthermore, the beginning teacher should not make an issue of the changes which he finds necessary. He must learn to be patient with his program and work consistently to bring about gradual improvements.

Many of the tensions between today's teachers result from the roles they assume while working closely with fellow teachers in a team effort. This can be illustrated by the disagreements described in this chapter regarding the art and language teachers. A study at the University of Texas Research and Development Center[7] has revealed that the conflicts often result between the "in-group" and the "out-group." The study found that the novice teacher who joins a team is less likely to experience difficulties when he yields to the older team members on issues which he feels are logically tenuous or psychologically threatening. This does not suggest that he must remain docile, but that he choose a time to assert himself when he is sure of support from members of the dominant group. Can this also be true when teachers work individually but in the same physical or academic area? The research does not say, but it appears logical that some of the same principles might be valid. Perhaps some difficulties in faculty relations are caused when newer professionals fail to understand the process by which their ideas will be more likely perceived.

Since teachers spend most of their time with students, they often find themselves out of contact with school administrators and other teachers. They often feel a need to be able to discuss

[6]R. L. Geiser, "I'd Like To Change Things, But. . .," *Illinois Teacher* 90:25-67, October, 1972.

[7]J. Gallesich, "Team Teaching Study of Team Division and Inter-Personal Functioning" *National Elementary Principal* 51:41-47, October, 1971.

their concerns and frustrations with colleagues and with the principal or deans. The need appears to be especially strong in large schools where teachers may teach all year without learning the names of many of their counterparts. At least one principal has begun to do something to improve the situation.

While principal of a California high school, Dr. Edward Weber was so concerned with opening the lines of communications among teachers that a Period Conference Seminar is used in which the principal spends his entire day in the conference room and with each teacher, counselor, and administrator who come for one period during the day[8]. The climate is relaxed, informal, and the discussion progresses from a general to a specific aspect of school life or curriculum that the principal or faculty members have singled out for discussion, such as ability grouping, school drug problems, and grading. The resulting remarks of participating teachers provide some insight into some of the causes of faculty relations problems:

"We feel that what we have to say is important and that it has a bearing on the ultimate decision of the group."

"The opportunity to know the principal on a more personal and friendly basis has made me more willing to seek his counsel."

"The seminars open up lines of communication. Hearing different points of view is a broadening experience. It beats after school meetings!"

This report indicates how a building administrator establishes effective relationships with teachers. However, a close examination of his procedure may indicate that similar procedures could possibly be effective for teachers and teaching candidates.

The experts suggest that effective faculty relations involve dimensions ranging from an individual's attempt to work with another individual to conscious programs which deliberately encourage effective faculty communications. Try to determine what is and what is not working in the schools you know and decide what you can do to develop your capacity to work congenially with colleagues.

[8]E. J. Weber, "Strangers In the Hallways," *Clearing House* 46: 141-2, Nov., 1971.

## DISCUSSION OF QUESTIONS

### Choose Your Side and Stand Your Ground

1. *What seems to have caused the conflict?* The teachers could not keep their differences at a philosophical level.

2. *Can we say that Mrs. Newley's teaching style was better than Mrs. Teal's?* Not on the basis of what is known. In order to make a definitive case, Mrs. Newley would have to produce some supportive evidence to show that her type of teaching is superior.

3. *Why must the present situation not be allowed?* Teachers who work closely together are expected to have differences in opinion, yet they must not permit the disagreements to damage their effectiveness as teachers. Now that the differences have surfaced so much that they are being noticed by the students, they must be controlled in order to prevent further embarrassment.

### There Is No Art in Envy

1. *What was the one unprofessional behavior which was seen more than once in the relationship of these two teachers?* Mrs. Creighton confronted Mrs. Bryce in the presence of her students. This practice causes many conflicts among faculty members. Because this is disturbing to students and can affect the teacher-teacher rapport and teacher-pupil rapport, it should not occur.

2. *Mrs. Creighton must not receive all of the blame since it was an action of Mrs. Bryce which initiated the entire development. What was that and how could it have been avoided?* Mrs. Bryce should not have corrected a student of another teacher. Instead, she should have reported what she saw directly to Mrs. Creighton.

### Encounter in the Lounge

1. *What assumptions are made by Mr. Kester in regard to sex roles within the school?* He assumes that there are some positions that only men can perform, and that the position of principal is one of them. He also seems to believe that women generally tend to impose on men and hold the profession back financially.

2. *What valid point has been made by the women?* Perhaps

the most valid point is that women are capable, but have not been given a chance to demonstrate that capability in responsible positions.

3. *What are some of the underlying issues that confront men and women in regard to faculty relations?* Certainly the status of women has to be considered. Salary is another issue that could emerge. The case also might point to the fact that the method of how a school is operated and controlled is also at stake.

## A Matter of Communication

1. *How can you explain (not justify) Mr. Hunt's feelings about the equipment?* He was an experienced teacher who had undoubtedly known the frustration of trying to teach without appropriate aids. Therefore, he may have become overly possessive of it, and yet he attempted to appear to colleagues that he was willing to share the devices. The participant may have become a convenient scapegoat.

2. *Did Ms. Carter act unprofessionally in lending the equipment?* Apparently not. She first proceeded unaware of any problem and she subsequently was involved in a situation where two teachers had different perceptions of the same incident. She used her judgment and felt that no parties would be inconvenienced.

3. *Suggest one way in which participants or teachers may be able to communicate with teachers or supervisors whose directions are difficult to comprehend.* Written communication is often an effective way to create understandings. If agreements are written and approved by both parties, some problems may be eliminated.

## The Grade Is Not the Same

1. *State one conclusion that can be drawn from the conflict that resulted in this case.* The student teacher assumed that he was delegated more authority than the teacher felt she had given.

2. *Who should have the authority to make the final decision?*

61

Since the teacher has the responsibility for the class, she must have the final authority.

3. *How can such incidents be prevented in the future?* This should serve as a signal to both the participant and the teacher that the lines of responsibility are not clearly defined. A substantive conference should follow which would more specifically define the participant's role.

| | A G R E E E | D I S A G R E E E | U N D E C I D E D |
|---|---|---|---|
| **POST-ASSESSMENT** | | | |

### How do you feel?

1. Most schools have harmonious faculties. — — —

2. The teaching profession is strengthened when men and women work together as equals. — — —

3. There is a pronounced pro-male sex role bias in our schools. — — —

4. Teachers who cannot get along with other teachers should be dismissed. — — —

5. Once a teacher makes a decision, he should stick by it even though it may have been a poor one, because admitting the error would lose the respect of his colleagues. — — —

### What do you think?

1. Teachers who have interpersonal conflicts with their colleagues are usually inconsiderate and self-centered. — — —

2. A teacher who finds himself in constant conflict with other teachers is probably at fault. — — —

3. If a fellow teacher purposefully annoys you, you should inform him in a diplomatic way before the annoyance becomes a conflict. — — —

4. When a teaching candidate is assigned definite responsibilities, he should have every right and authority enjoyed by his supervising teacher. — — —

5. Teachers who have more interpersonal problems with fellow teachers also have difficulty making their lessons effective. — — —

63

## SELF-ASSESSMENT:

Now that you have completed the post-assessment, compare your pre-and post-assessment scores. Check those questions for which there is disagreement between the two scores.

Examine your reasons for changing your responses. When possible, cite the specific reason which caused your change of opinion.

1. What should a teacher do when he feels that a supervisor or superior is being unfair?

2. How much real authority does a supervisor or superior have over a teacher or student teacher?

3. What guidelines can be established for promoting harmonious relationships with colleagues?

## FURTHER INVOLVEMENT

BURDIN, JOEL, Editor, *Journal of Teacher Education* 26:4, Winter, 1975.
The entire journal is devoted to the theme, "The Molding of the Nonsexist Teacher." The articles present different views and research information regarding the problem of sex roles in schools ranging from leadership positions to sex role stereotyping in the schools. Be sure to complete the checklist on p. 316 which rates your contribution to the elimination of sexism in schools.

BURNWORTH, JOE, "A Lunch to Remember," *The Teacher Educator* 7:3, Spring, 1972, pp. 14-17.
A lunch with the teachers gives the student teacher a lot of confusing ideas about teaching. Watch different teacher personalities emerge as they relate to each other. How many hang-ups and insecurities can you identify?

COLETTA, ANTHONY J., "Do Open and Traditional Teachers Differ in Their Beliefs About Learning?" *Phi Delta Kappan* 55: 636-7, May, 1974.
Do open and traditional teachers hold significantly different beliefs about how learning best occurs? This report specifies some of the differences and cites characteristics which will help you identify an open or traditional teacher when you meet one.

HINCKLEY, WILLIAM L., "Boiler Room Syndrome," *School and Community* 60:23, March, 1974.
Regardless of where the coffee pot is located, the personal interactions which take place in this communications center are likely to have a marked effect on the teachers who meet there. The boiler room syndrome is a phenomena that the teacher candidate should get to know. Read this, and then get up enough courage to visit the communications center of the next school you are in.

YEE, ALBERT H., "Are the Schools a Feminized Society?" *Educational Leadership* 31:128-33, November, 1973.
Examines the idea that schools reflect female biases. An excellent summary with many facts and a few surprises. A must for your next discussion concerning analysis of the type of people who become teachers.

# SECTION II

# BECOMING INVOLVED WITH STUDENTS IN THE CLASSROOM

## Chapter Four

## CLASSROOM CONFRONTATIONS

| | AGREEE | DISAGREE | UNDECIDED |
|---|---|---|---|

**PRE-ASSESSMENT**

*How do you feel?*

1. Today's students are generally not serious about academic tasks. — — —

2. The imposition of strict behavior codes causes pupils to feel alienated. — — —

3. A good classroom is a quiet classroom. — — —

4. A teacher should initially gain control of his class by being strict; he can relax his standards after he has established authority over the group. — — —

5. There are times when subject matter is more important than pupils. — — —

*What do you think?*

1. Corporal punishment consists of inflicting some type of physical abuse upon a student. — — —

2. The basic idea concerning the concept of successful discipline is to treat all students the same. — — —

3. Corporal punishment can only be administered legally by a designated official in the school. — — —

4. The teacher's task is to transmit information; the pupil's responsibility is to apprehend what is taught. — — —

5. The use of paddling rests on the assumption that pain is a motivating force. — — —

# INTRODUCTION

It has long been known that the school is an intellectual institution, but recent critics have pointed out that cognitive processes alone are not enough. The school is a place where people learn to interact with each other. It is where feelings, beliefs, values, attitudes, and emotions are displayed and examined. The constant interplay between students and teachers frequently leads to problems in human relations.

If the affective climate (the emotional relationship between teacher and pupils) is characterized by warmth, concern, understanding, and empathy, favorable benefits should result both for the teacher and students. If it is manifested by fear, alienation, frustration, and selfishness, negative behaviors will have to be contended with.

The results of teacher-pupil interaction in the classroom are as real as the outcomes from formal academic study. Although the teacher is affected by his perception of the class and its collective behavior, he is in the better position to manipulate the environment so that certain types of behaviors, feelings, and attitudes have a good opportunity to emerge. Overt displays of hostility or resentment by pupils may be only surface expressions designed to conceal uncomfortable underlying feelings. The teacher, however, may perceive such displays as aggressive behavior which is designed to challenge his authority.

The following incidents present situations where teacher feelings and student feelings come into conflict. We hope that the reader can discover insights into how these situations develop and how a teacher can not only cope with them, but modify them, creating an atmosphere where the most positive kinds of human relationships can develop.

## IN THE CLASSROOM

### Mr. Angelo's Dilemma

During his field experience, Mr. Angelo was scheduled to teach three classes. The fourth and sixth period groups seemed cooperative and eager to learn, but the third period class contained several students who collectively were negative toward both teacher and school.

Even if Mr. Angelo had known of the third period situation, it probably would not have affected his teaching procedure, for he already had fixed ideas about rapport and classroom climate. He felt that he could command respect by identifying with the students and being "one of the guys." He rejected the practice of strict discipline because he was opposed to corporal punishment. He sincerely wanted to avoid the insecure feeling that he feared would develop if he subjected his class to stringent corrective measures.

Problems started the very first day. Several pupils in his third period class sat in the back of the room and talked while he was lecturing; a few boys made various types of noises; still others walked around while the class was in session. His lengthy, straight-from-the-book lectures, in the same monotonous voice tone only made matters worse. When he failed to enforce his repeated threats of detention for those who did not comply with his demands, the situation continued to deteriorate.

Mr. Angelo's future as a teacher was at stake. So was the education of his students.

#### Becoming Involved

1. Could you say that the root of Mr. Angelo's problem was a general lack of concern?

2. What was wrong with the manner in which threats were used?

3. Should Mr. Angelo have been more strict initially and later established the type of climate that he liked?

4. Was the dislike for corporal punishment a weakness?

### Field Exploration

If you have an opportunity to actually teach a class, try different teaching styles and observe the results. First, try an approach similar to Mr. Angelo's for a few minutes. What happens to the students? Then try a technique which has more enthusiasm and which involves student participation. Is there a difference in student response? Does teacher behavior influence pupil behavior?

## Learning by the Board

The first few weeks at Stonewall High School were delightful. The students were well-dressed, well-mannered, and cooperative. Some of the older teachers said that "recess" was going to end very soon, but Mr. Hanes thought he could cope with any situation here.

About midway through the second month of school, some of the rather spirited students began to be more boisterous. Mr. Hanes did not want to jeopardize his good relationship with them, so he tried to overlook the incidents assuming that they would subside. Instead of diminishing, they multiplied and Mr. Hanes soon realized that he would be compelled to take action before the situation worsened. At first he tried keeping the troublesome students after school and requiring them to write extra reports. He often directed sarcastic remarks to individuals, but this only caused more contention.

Some of the older teachers repeatedly advised Mr. Hanes to try corporal punishment instead, explaining that the best way to gain the respect and control of his classes was by physical means. He was opposed to this because of his belief that corporal punishment is more harmful than beneficial. Instead of administering physical chastisement, he sent the annoying students to the principal's office. Much to Hanes' surprise, Mr. Nelson, the principal, brought the troublesome group back to his class and told him to administer his own discipline and suggested that more forceful methods might help. Mr. Hanes was still reluctant to go this far. His next attempt was to have disruptive students stand in the hall just outside the room. This failed to improve the situation, but it seemed to be the only remaining available option.

The climax occurred on Wednesday when one of the boys, Dennis Brandon, decided to light a cigarette in class. Mr. Hanes ordered him to discontinue smoking and to go out into the hall. Moments later, there was a disturbance outside the door. Mr. Hanes rushed from his room and found Mr. McDaniel, a physical education teacher, paddling Dennis, who apparently had continued to smoke. After school, Mr. Hanes was called to the principal's office, where Mr. Nelson told him that a teacher who could not alleviate his own classroom problems did not belong on the school staff. "If your situation fails to improve," he continued, "I will have no alternative but to secure a different teacher next year."

Mr. Hanes was not so much concerned with the next year as he was with the next day. When a student misbehaved--and one surely would--what was he going to do?

### Becoming Involved

1. Was Mr. Hanes' basic problem a lack of willingness to experiment with various approaches?

2. Should a teacher ever take responsibility for disciplining a student who is in another teacher's class?

3. Mr. Hanes' problem with the Stonewall faculty and staff was based on an underlying difference in philosophy regarding corporal punishment. What should he do?

4. Was the principal justified in refusing to handle discipline problems?

5. Why did the use of sarcasm fail?

6. If Mr. Hanes' extra assignments had reduced the problems, should he adopt this method as a permanent approach?

### Field Exploration

Talk with a dean of boys or with a principal concerning the execution of corporal punishment. Who is responsible? Is it effective? What conditions must exist before a pupil may be paddled? Ask what the administrator considers to be his role in seeing that

71

students behave satisfactorily and classroom climate is maintained. Does he feel that the teacher should basically be able to solve most of the problems that occur in a classroom?

Compare your notes with those of the other students and compile a list of options that are available for teachers to use in coping with students whose behavior is disruptive.

### Hassle in the Hot Box

Tom Johnson, a new participant at Central High, found a most revealing situation when he paid a visit to Ms. Schilling's class. The first thing he noticed was that students were still conversing in the hall after the bell rang. When all except two boys were finally in their seats, the teacher began to call the roll. A murmur ran through the class as she spoke each name and received the unfailing "here" or "present."

"Now pass in your homework for today," said Ms. Schilling. People began to talk, and many of the papers did not arrive at the front of the class. Those which did arrive came by many routes. The exasperated teacher moved swiftly along each row of seats, picking up the missing assignments from the desks.

By the middle of the period, the room temperature had reached a very uncomfortable level. Several students became drowsy, and three boys rested their heads on their desks. A student raised a window, letting a chilling blast of February air into the uncomfortable room.

"Close the window right now," snapped Ms. Schilling. Reluctantly, the boy obeyed.

After a prolonged lecture and discussion period, the teacher declared that the remaining ten minutes would be for study, but she gave no further instructions. As soon as Ms. Schilling had made the announcement, four youths sauntered over to the pencil sharpener.

During the so-called study time, one student came to Ms. Schilling's desk to ask a question. Before the student moved away, another pupil stood at the desk waiting for her question to be

72

answered. Within five minutes several more individuals crowded around seeking help and obscuring the teacher's view of the class. Just when it appeared that the class might get completely out of control, the bell rang and the group filed out without a final word from their teacher.

### Becoming Involved

1. What evidence is there that Ms. Schilling was poorly organized?

2. How does the lack of defined systematic routine affect students?

3. Was it unwise for the teacher to talk to individual students?

4. How could Ms. Schilling have alleviated the problems in the class?

### Field Exploration

During your next class observation, write down the directions which a teacher gives. What seems to be successful in securing student cooperation?

### How Far Can a Grasshopper Fly?

Mr. Sloan, a new student teacher at South High School, thought the fifth period history class was going to be fun to teach. He observed that Miss Warner, his supervising teacher, held the attention of the class, and he expected that the students would cooperate with him, too.

He was well prepared for his first presentation. Although the students were orderly, they kept asking him foolish questions such as, "How far can a grasshopper fly without stopping?" He admitted that he did not know, and hypothesized that the students were trying to see how far they could push him because he was a "naive" beginner.

As the weeks progressed, Mr. Sloan seemed to gain the respect of the class. They apparently liked him because they were friendly and cooperative. He felt that he had established good rapport while maintaining a suitable learning climate.

Near the end of the student teaching experience, the class began to think of giving him a going-away party. He did not really want such a celebration, but Miss Warner granted permission for the festivity. Some of the students told him that they were going to bring liquor to the party. He responded by telling them they would be in trouble if they did anything like that.

On the day of the party, there was a generous amount of food and soft drinks. Mr. Sloan noticed that some of the beverage bottles were filled unusually close to the top. He took one from Charles, smelled it, and then sipped it. It had the unmistakable taste of whiskey. Many students had already started drinking and Mr. Sloan was in a quandary. What would happen if their conduct became unruly or if school administrative personnel should become aware that students were drinking at school?

## Becoming Involved

1. What was the first clue that these students were departing from the teacher's leadership?

2. To whom did Mr. Sloan have to answer for his mistakes?

3. Since Mr. Sloan forbade the students to bring the liquor, was he actually responsible for their behavior?

## Field Exploration

Field experiences place the teaching candidate in a position of having teacher responsibilities while still being a student. Talk to a student who has recently completed his clinical assignment and ask about this vulnerable predicament. Then talk to a supervising teacher and determine how he assists student participants when conflicts arise.

74

**Friday Slides**

Miss Simpson felt that informal, student-centered classrooms were best, and she avoided any temptation to punish students. She made every effort to tolerate the actions and remarks from the boys in the back row, thinking that calling attention to them would only complicate matters. Although most of the class did not appear to be bothered, there were some serious students who felt they were being cheated because the clique in the back row was too noisy. They complained to Miss Simpson, but she assumed the students would eventually become more subdued. Consequently, she said nothing to them except for an occasional "Would you become more quiet, please?" This was effective only for a few minutes at a time, but she was determined not to lose her cool.

On this particular Friday, Miss Simpson was showing slides of famous people in history who had been alienated by society. During the presentation, she was preoccupied with operating the projector, and was only faintly aware of the paper tearing, laughing, and other confusion in the room. When the presentation was over, she attempted unsuccessfully to have the class discuss the impact of the slides. Since this approach failed, she had them write a paper on the discussion topic thinking this would be one method of quelling the class.

When the session ended, Miss Simpson began reading the student comments and discovered that several persons were accusing the boys in the back row of throwing objects at the people in the front of the room during the slide presentation. One student had complained about being hit several times. Others said that the situation should be reported to the dean if the unruly students were not brought under control.

### Becoming Involved

1. Often when the teacher is too strict, the students retaliate. Is this what had happened in Miss Simpson's class?

2. What poor communication skills were found in Miss Simpson's teaching?

3. Miss Simpson wanted her classes to have an informal, relaxed atmosphere. Is this good?

4. Was this class really too noisy?

### Field Exploration

Your field experiences should provide opportunity for you to visit more than one school. If so, compare the degrees of student freedom between two schools.

If your visits are restricted to one school, try to visit several classes. Closely observe students to see if they really perceive what is expected of them. See if those rooms are quieter or louder than in situations where the expectations are more vague.

### Panic at Ten O'Clock

Since Rick had been doing so well during his first few weeks of clinical experience, his supervisor asked him if he wanted to assume responsibility for homeroom supervision for the remaining weeks. He was quick to point out that it was considered to be an "undesirable" homeroom and that if there were any doubts about being able to control the class, it would be better if he rejected the offer. Rick accepted because he knew it would be good experience.

As the ten o'clock hour approached, Rick began to wonder what was meant by "undesirable." Mr. Cohen explained that his homeroom contained 25 freshmen and that four or five of that group were the school's habitual problem students. This concerned Rick, but not enough to discourage him from wanting to supervise the group.

Mr. Cohen continued, "The rest of the class is all right if you can control the four or five. If they get out of hand, the whole class will follow their lead and then you will have problems. Still want it?"

"More than ever!" Rick said.

"All right, I will get the attendance sheet and the daily announcements ready for you. Good luck."

When the second period ended, Rick was as tense as he had been on his first day at the school. As he walked down the hall toward the homeroom, he showed visible symptoms of stress.

When he entered the room, some of the students wanted to know who he was and what he was doing there. Gradually they settled into their seats. When the bell sounded, the noise level in the room failed to subside making it almost impossible to take attendance.

None of the students had brought books to read, so Rick distributed some magazines. He asked the group to be quiet, but a few students continued talking and laughing. He proceeded to disperse the troublesome ones into different sections of the room hoping that isolation would help. He then tried to think of what Mr. Cohen would do in a situation like this and concluded that he never would have let it get out of hand in the first place.

The students began sailing paper airplanes and pitching materials across the room. Rick told them to pick up all the trash on the floor. They did, but they only tossed it about the room again. Two boys began scuffling in the back of the room. There was only temporary success in stopping it.

"Everybody listen! There is going to be order in this room!", Rick shouted. He began moving students around and it became extremely quiet as he ordered the offenders to pick up the paper. But, just as the situation seemed to be under control, a few pupils began to taunt him again. The assemblage immediately followed their lead and were as noisy as ever. As he became more vociferous, the clamor in the room increased.

"This is what Mr. Cohen meant by 'undesirable'," Rick was thinking. "What can I do now?"

## Becoming Involved

1. From Rick's behavior, what can we say about his general attitude?

2. What steps did Rick take in attempting to control the troublesome behavior?

3. What advantage is there to knowing in advance that certain students may cause trouble?

4. What disadvantages are there to knowing in advance that certain students may cause trouble?

5. Should a teacher single out the boisterous students and reprimand them?

## Field Exploration

Today many teachers feel that homerooms are unnecessary. Visit one or two homerooms and record the teacher's technique in relating to the students. Compare this with similar observations made by your peers; then make a list of the purposes and problems presented by homerooms.

### Those Youth Should Understand

Mr. Stanton slowly read a note which had been placed in his mailbox:

> *Dear Mr. Stanton:*
> *A very important meeting will be held today at 3:15*
> *p.m. in my office. This meeting is of major importance*
> *to you, so please be there.*
>
> *Fred Rison, Principal*

He folded the note and slipped it into his pocket. As he walked down the hall to class, he thought about the possible reasons for this important conference. Why was it called so suddenly? Why was it of such major importance to him?

Aroused from his thoughts by the final bell, Mr. Stanton hurriedly collected the test papers. He was then surrounded by students who complained about the fact that he had not explained some of the questions and problems that were on the test. Mr. Stanton left the room at the end of the period and moved through the throng to his last period study hall still somewhat annoyed by the accusations.

After attendance check was completed, he began to grade some of the tests. There were a number of D's and even quite a few F's, but he was sure that he was not responsible. What could he do? He had presented the facts. It was up to them to learn what he had taught.

As the hands on the clock moved closer to 3:00, he thought about the meeting and concluded that it had been called because many of the parents were unhappy with his teaching.

Mrs. Jordan had recently criticized him for the "F" he had assigned to her son, complaining that he had given him no help. She could not understand why he refused to give individual assistance in a class of only fifteen.

He then recalled that Mrs. Parker had denounced him because he had not given help to her daughter when she had specifically requested it. The indignant mother had remarked that she did not like having her daughter come home with the news that her teacher had called her and some of the other students "stupid and irresponsible."

Mr. Stanton was convinced that this was what the meeting was about. Yes, he had confronted the students, but he actually *did* think they were stupid and irresponsible, in a way. He failed to understand why he must explain every little detail to all of his classes. After all, they were in high school. Why couldn't they comprehend simple facts and ideas? It certainly was not all his fault!

Mr. Stanton was brought back to reality by the 3:05 dismissal bell. He gathered his papers and walked to the office where he was greeted by Mr. Rison, who told him that there were a number of parents who had requested a conference regarding his teaching. He followed him into the conference room. The door gently closed.

79

### Becoming Involved

1. What did Mr. Stanton actually do which suggests that he felt superior to his students?
2. What obvious faults did he display?
3. Does a behavior, such as the one demonstrated in this case, tend to create an environment of alienation or resentment?
4. What was Mr. Stanton's greatest weakness?

### Field Exploration

It should not take an observer long to detect a few students who seem to have difficulty with comprehension of subject matter. Talk with a few and ask what a teacher could do to help them better understand what is going on in the class. You might also ask what method some teachers employ to make learning easier.

This conversation may also lead to the opportunity to discuss what kinds of teachers are best liked. How do they respond to teachers who take a superior attitude and do not understand why it is so hard to learn concepts?

## WHAT THE EXPERTS SAY

Confrontations seem to result when the goals of teachers and the goals of students are in conflict. Why does this happen? Who is responsible? What methods successfully prevent or reduce confrontations? Several interesting ideas have been expressed by people who have studied problems of this type.

According to public opinion as measured by the Gallup Poll,[1] lack of discipline has been consistently mentioned as the chief problem in the schools. In addition, the public seems to favor sending children to a school that has strict discipline, a strict dress code, and places emphasis on the three R's. In other words, the public seems to favor a traditional, highly-disciplined school setting. Confrontations, consequently, may frequently be the result

[1]George Gallup, "Seventh Annual Gallup Poll of Public Attitudes Toward Education," *Phi Delta Kappan* 57:4, pp 227-241, December, 1975.

of students' reacting both to the philosophies of their parents and their teachers.

Many authorities believe that a teacher's style considerably affects the performance of a class. One investigation assessed the effects of behavioral objectives, criterion evaluation, and remediation upon the classroom progress of disruptive students. Two eighth-grade teachers were taught to utilize the above techniques under controlled conditions. It was concluded that the use of behavioral objectives, criterion evaluation, and remediation had a positive effect on the classroom progress of disruptive adolescents.[2] The research seems to indicate that more sophisticated procedures may be of some value in controlling a disruptive class.

The administration of corporal punishment has taken a completely new perspective due to the Baker vs. Owen[3] decision in the Supreme Court in October, 1975. The court affirmed the right of teachers and principals to administer corporal punishment because they have a legitimate and substantial interest in maintaining order and discipline in the schools. Therefore, the court concluded, force is reasonable and school officials are free to employ corporal punishment.

Perhaps the most significant implication of the court's ruling is the fact that they determined that procedural due process now applies to corporal punishment. The case resulted in four principles governing the use of corporal punishment:

1. Corporal punishment should not be used unless the student was forewarned that specific misbehavior would cause its use.

2. Corporal punishment "should never be employed as a first line of punishment for misbehavior."

3. Corporal punishment can only be administered in the company of a second staff member who has been informed beforehand and in the student's presence of the reason for the punishment."

[2]A. Bert Webb, and William H. Cormier, "Improving Classroom Behavior and Discipline," *Journal of Experimental Education* 41:2, Winter, 1972, 92-96.
[3]Thomas J. Flygare, "Procedural Due Process Now Applies to Corporal Punishment," *Phi Delta Kappan* 57:5, January, 1976, pp. 345-346.

4. If the parents so request, the official who administered the punishment must furnish a written statement of the reasons for using this form of punishment.

The Supreme Court, then, has reaffirmed the use of corporal punishment, but it has very specifically defined the conditions under which it can be administered. Some educational and legal personnel are suggesting that this case may signal the ultimate end of the use of corporal punishment in the schools because of the determination that due process must be exercised.

Many educators, however, still feel that paddling is an effective method of enforcing student cooperation and they will probably continue its use. Although this approach is popular in many circles, several extensive investigations seem to parallel the findings of Vredervoe's study[4] of students and school discipline. The major results indicated that:

1. Corporal punishment is a means of dealing with symptoms, not the cause.

2. Those usually given corporal punishment are used to it and, as a result, it has little deterrent effect.

3. Corporal punishment and teaching as a profession do not belong together.

4. Expulsion or segregation has greater effect on the student than corporal punishment.

5. Corporal punishment is usually employed by those who should not be permitted to use it. They seek to eliminate or control a problem rather than to solve it.

Other experts[5] believe that "instructional needs are served when the teacher defines, reasonably and unemotionally, the limits of classroom behavior."

Several of the cases in this chapter would be described by the observer as unruly situations. Keene[6] suggests some ways of coping with an unruly class.

[4]Laurence E. Vredervoe, "School Discipline Third Report on a Study of Students and School Discipline in the United States and Other Countries," *Bulletin of the National Association of Secondary School Principals* 49:215-216, March, 1965.

[5]Fritz Redl and William W. Wattenberg, *Mental Hygiene in Teaching,* New York: Harcourt Brace and Co., 1959, pp. 361-362.

[6]Melvin Keene, *Beginning Secondary School Teachers Guide,* New York; Harper and Row, 1969.

1. Be friendly but firm, and avoid developing a punitive approach.

2. At the slightest evidence of a disorderly student's attempt to disorganize your class, be stern.

3. Do not turn your back on an unruly class.

4. Be careful not to make false accusations of misconduct.

5. Put the welfare of the class first and insist that students do the same.

6. Be certain that every student participates in the lesson.

7. Strive to remain calm and confident.

How does a teacher cope with disruptive behavior and create a humane environment? Many people argue that rough and threatening behavior is the only way to gain control. A section on discipline by B. O. Smith in the *Encyclopedia of Educational Research*[7] refutes this idea and submits that rough and threatening behavior on the part of the teacher may actually be part of the cause. Do we sometimes provide fuel for the fire when we are actually attempting to control the blaze?

The process of teaching involves the successful interaction between the teacher and students. Smith[8] describes the teaching cycle as the sequential process of interaction between teacher and learner which consists of the teacher's perceiving, diagnosing, and reacting to the pupil, who in turn, perceives, diagnoses, and reacts to the teacher. Thus, negative behavior by the teacher may initiate a negative cycle. The experts express the notion that successful teaching involves constant constructive interaction between teacher and class with the teacher making conscious effort to help students learn.

## DISCUSSION OF QUESTIONS

### Mr. Angelo's Dilemma

1. *Could you say that the root of Mr. Angelo's problems was a general lack of concern?* No. The fact that he had decided on a

[7]B. Othanel Smith, "Discipline," *Encyclopedia of Educational Research*, 4th Edition, New York; Macmillan Co., 1969, p. 296.
[8]B. Othanel Smith, "A Concept of Teaching," *Language and Concepts in Education*, Chicago: Rand McNally, 1961, Chapter 6.

definite strategy before his first day of teaching suggests that he was acutely concerned with his relationships with the students.

2. *What was wrong with the manner in which threats were used?* He made threats but apparently never followed through. Pupils soon learned not to take him seriously.

3. *Should Mr. Angelo have been more strict initially and later established the type of climate that he liked?* The old adage "It's always better to begin by being strict, for you can always relax later" is highly questionable. While firmness, assertion, and consistency are most important, excessive authority is likely to provoke the students into a silent or open revolt.

4. *Was the dislike for corporal punishment a weakness?* No. Although this concern may have been partially responsible for his dilemma, his continuing dislike for severe punishment will probably stimulate him to find more desirable methods for establishing the needed rapport with his students.

## Learning by the Board

1. *Was Mr. Hanes' basic problem a lack of willingness to experiment with various approaches?* No. He tried extra assignments, sending students outside, sarcasm, verbal reprimand, and keeping them after school. Perhaps the basic problem was that they were all punitive measures.

2. *Should a teacher ever take responsibility for disciplining a student who is in another teacher's class?* Generally not, because this reflects the other teacher's failure to work things out with his students and can lead to unnecessary conflicts among teachers.

3. *Mr. Hanes' problem with the Stonewall faculty and staff was based on an underlying difference in philosophy regarding corporal punishment. What should he do?* Since Mr. Hanes seems to be getting little or no useful information from his colleagues, he should consult the literature for research on discipline. His investigation could include teaching methods, textbooks, professional education journals, and the *Review of Educational Research*. He should continue experimenting with non-physical approaches.

4. *Was the principal justified in refusing to handle discipline problems?* In a sense he was. A principal has so many administrative responsibilities that he does not have an unlimited amount of time to spend disciplining students. He should be asked to help only in rare cases where the teacher finds an especially difficult situation.

5. *Why did the use of sarcasm fail?* Sarcasm may be a successful procedure for forcing some students to concede, but it may have the opposite effect on others and thus provoke further misbehavior. Because sarcasm is directed to the student as a person rather than at his behavior, it has the potential of doing permanent damage to his emotional well-being. By humiliating a student, the teacher may teach him to dislike the school, the teacher, and worst of all, himself.

6. *Suppose Mr. Hanes' extra assignments had reduced the problems. Should he adopt this method as a permanent approach?* When schoolwork of any type is used for punishment, it may instill a dislike for study in spite of the fact that it initially appears to be successful.

### Hassle in the Hot Box

1. *What evidence is there that Ms. Schilling was poorly organized?* She had failed to adjust the room thermostat; she had no organized system for collecting student homework; she continued to call the roll while students simultaneously talked; the students did not get permission and wait their turn to answer questions; most of the students were not ready to work when the bell rang; several students gathered around the pencil sharpener; and she apparently finished the lesson material before the hour ended without having further planned activities.

2. *How does the lack of defined systematic routine affect students?* It usually has the results found in Ms. Schilling's classes. Students are left confused and the confusion rapidly changes to lack of interest.

3. *Was it unwise for the teacher to talk to individual students?* While teachers should give some attention in class to individuals, they cannot afford to do so for a prolonged time, ignoring the rest of the class.

4. *How could Ms. Schilling have alleviated the problems in the class?* She could have planned a lesson which is sufficiently long, made more specific directions for study, and given attention to the uncomfortable room temperature.

### How Far Can A Grasshopper Fly?

1. *What was the first clue that these students were departing from the teacher's leadership?* The students were asking inane and irrelevant questions in an attempt to lure his attention from the lesson.

2. *To whom did Mr. Sloan have to answer for his mistakes?* As a student teacher, he was directly responsible to his supervising teacher and his college supervisor. In a broader sense, he also has to account for his behavior to other professionals.

3. *Since Mr. Sloan forbade the students to bring the liquor, was he actually responsible for their behavior?* He was teaching the class at the time. The teacher is responsible for the behavior of students in his classes whether he is in the room or not.

### Friday Slides

1. *Often when the teacher is too strict, the students retaliate. Is this what had happened in Miss Simpson's class?* Definitely not. Miss Simpson had been aware of the potential breakdown in discipline in this class for some time. Yet, she had refrained from the temptation to become stern. Her behavior suggests that she really preferred an unstructured atmosphere over a strict, dictatorial climate.

2. *What poor communication skills were found in Miss Simpson's teaching?* During the media presentation, she directed her attention to the slides rather than to the students. Also, she

should have involved them in some way; possibly preventing some of the events that occurred.

3. *Miss Simpson wanted her classes to have an informal, relaxed atmosphere. Is this good?* Yes. The optimal working conditions are when students are relaxed. However, any student's degree of freedom should end when it reaches the point of disturbing other students.

4. *Was this class really too noisy?* The continuous complaints from students indicate that there was too much confusion. However, a busy class sometimes is noisy. One must assess the actual progress being made before a definite answer can be given.

## Panic at Ten O'Clock

1. *From Rick's behavior, what can we say about his general attitude?* His eagerness to accept a homeroom which had a reputation for being difficult indicates courage on Rick's behalf. His trying several approaches suggests that he is aware of the need to experiment with different techniques of control.

2. *What steps did Rick take in attempting to control the troublesome behavior?* He provided students with reading materials, separated the problem group, told students to pick up their papers from the floor, and finally shouted at them.

3. *What advantage is there to knowing in advance that certain students may cause trouble?* It allows the teacher to plan activities to involve these students and capture their interests.

4. *What disadvantages are there to knowing that certain students may cause trouble?* Teachers often stereotype students as "troublemakers." If you already have this image in your mind when one of those individuals first enters your room, you are apt to treat him as you think an agitator deserves to be dealt with. This encourages him to fight back. The practice of stereotyping students is unhealthy because the teacher's image of a student is sooner or later transferred to him. Once he sees himself as an agitator he feels a need to live up to this self image.

5. *Should a teacher single out the boisterous students and reprimand them?* If reproof is needed, it should be given in pri-

vate. Public rebuke provides attention for students who disrupt. Since some students need more attention, they will play havoc with the class just to get recognition. Also, public chiding can be damaging to the attitudes and emotions of some students.

## Those Youth Should Understand

1. *What did Mr. Stanton actually do which suggests that he felt superior to his students?* He assigned a number of D's and F's. He refused to explain, even when students asked for help. He reportedly indicated that he thought them inferior people.

2. *What obvious faults did he display?* The test scores indicated that either he was an ineffective teacher or his testing skills were poor. He refused to help students who asked for assistance.

3. *Does a behavior, such as the one demonstrated in this case, tend to create an environment of alienation or resentment?* Since it is generally acknowledged that teacher behavior affects pupil behavior, it must be assumed that he is inviting confrontations instead of establishing a climate where students feel secure and accepted.

4. *What was Mr. Stanton's greatest weakness?* This is an easy question to ask, but difficult to answer. Probably Mr. Stanton's failure to recognize that a teacher should help students learn by providing a supportive environment was basic.

| | | D I S A G R E E E | U N D E C I D E D |
|---|---|---|---|

**POST-ASSESSMENT**

*How do you feel?*

1. Today's students are generally not serious about academic tasks. — — —

2. The imposition of strict behavior codes causes pupils to feel alienated. — — —

3. A good classroom is a quiet classroom. — — —

4. A teacher should initially gain control of his class by being strict; he can relax his standards after he has established authority over the group. — —

5. There are times when subject matter is more important than pupils. — — —

**What do you think?**

1. Corporal punishment consists of inflicting some type of physical abuse upon a student. — — —

2. The basic idea concerning the concept of successful discipline is to treat all students the same. — — —

3. Corporal punishment can only be administered legally by a designated official in the school. — — —

4. The teacher's task is to transmit information; the pupil's responsibility is to apprehend what is taught. — — —

5. The use of paddling rests on the assumption that pain is a motivating force. — — —

## SELF-ASSESSMENT:

Now that you have completed the post-assessment, compare your pre- and post-assessment scores. Check those items where there is disagreement between responses. Examine your reasons for any change. When possible, cite the specific rationale which caused your change of opinion.

1. What changes in knowledge were experienced from the study of classroom confrontations?

2. What changes in beliefs were experienced as a result of the analysis of the classroom incidents?

3. In your view, what are the most relevant concerns in establishing an effective classroom environment?

4. What do you know and believe about:
   a. The nature of students?
   b. The conditions which affect teacher and pupil behavior in the classroom?
   c. Discipline and corporal punishment?
   d. The causes of tension between teacher and students?

## FURTHER INVOLVEMENT

CARNOT, JOSEPH B., "Dynamic and Effective School Discipline," *Clearing House* 48:3, pp. 150-53, November, 1973.

This article analyzes the three most common approaches used by teachers to establish and maintain classroom discipline. The author then considers what must be done to insure good behavior in the classroom.

GEORGE, PAUL S., "Good Discipline Through Contingency Management," *Clearing House* 48:3, pp. 145-149, November, 1973.

The author considers methods for developing effective discipline and presents strategies designed for implementing discipline policy by teachers.

JONES, ALAN, *Students, Don't Push the Teachers Down the Stairs on Friday*, Baltimore, Penguin Books, Inc., 1973, 179 pp.

This book is about as subtle as a slap in the face. It only took Mr. Jones about five minutes to realize that his beliefs would not work here. Is this a jungle, or is it a school? Is the coach's style the only one that will work?

NATIONAL EDUCATION ASSOCIATION, *Report of the Task Force on Corporal Punishment,* The Association, Washington, D.C., 1972, 29 pp.

This report presents a series of findings and recommendations on the current situation in American schools regarding corporal punishment.

SCHULER, ALFRED, and SHEA, JOHN V., "The Discipline Game: Playing Without Losers," *Learning* 3.1, pp. 80-86, Aug./Sept., 1974.

Specific techniques are presented for improving strained relations between students and teachers.

## Chapter Five

## EMERGING STUDENT RIGHTS

| | A G R E E | D I S A G R E E | U N D E C I D E D |
|---|---|---|---|

### PRE-ASSESSMENT

*How do you feel?*

1. If students receive too many rights, there will be constant problems for the school. — — —

2. Students should not have the same prerogatives as adults because they are not mature enough to accept the accompanying responsibilities. — — —

3. When making decisions regarding student privileges, the teacher should give more consideration to the pupil's previous record than his "rights." — — —

4. Teacher rights should receive priority over student demands. — — —

5. Too many student rights have been granted too suddenly. — — —

### What do you think?

1. The individual liberties of citizens are not guaranteed to students who are under eighteen because, like a guardian, the school is responsible for their welfare. — — —

2. In case of suspension, the student has the right to be confronted with the evidence against him. — — —

3. A right in the broadest sense is more than a legal term. — — —

4. Students are now able to successfully contest teachers' decisions. — — —

5. Group rights supersede individual preferences in the classroom. — — —

92

## INTRODUCTION

Students today are securing more rights in schools than ever before. Motivated by an increased awareness and supported by recent court cases, the adolescent is more conscious than ever of the fact that he is not subjected to a system which he cannot change. The teacher-dominated, student-submissive concept is giving way to a shared relationship where both parties are more aware of extending basic freedoms into the classroom.

The increasing social awareness of the late 60's and early 70's has caused teachers and students alike to be cognizant of human rights which insure that each individual has dignity. He has the right to express his feelings without retribution, and he is probably now more comprehending of himself as a person than ever before.

Then one might ask why students have not always enjoyed these prerogatives. Perhaps the best answer is that until recently they were not as aware of their civil rights and, therefore, did not question the teacher's decision even when it seemed to eliminate some freedom. Another possible explanation is that parents and the general public believe that students have too many rights and privileges. This attitude undoubtedly has some impact upon student rights.

The legal rights of students are being identified more specifically by the courts. Decisions in regard to dress codes, hair styles, freedom of speech, and due process favor the student and indicate that he is entitled to the same considerations as an adult. Thus, as cases in this chapter will indicate, students may appear to be more demanding, and teachers and administrators may have to be more cautious or specific in their governance activities.

Today's teacher must prepare to cope with situations which might involve student rights. No longer can teachers use one set of standards for adults and another for adolescents. Teachers must be concerned with the constitutional and personal rights of students in every segment of the educational domain. Furthermore, many classroom situations will be the forum for the interpretation and improvement of the human condition. The opportunity to

93

dissent, for example, should be recognized and analyzed in the classroom setting. Hopefully it will not be an attorney who must act on behalf of the student. The teacher should be available and ready to help the student be aware of his rights and accompanying responsibilities.

How will you fulfill your obligations to students when you begin teaching? When reacting to the following situations, imagine yourself as the teacher and try to determine how you would respond to insure that all students have the rights which are guaranteed to them.

## IN THE CLASSROOM

### Innocent Until Proven Guilty

Butler High School was built forty years ago and was the showcase of educational institutions in the area for several years. Throughout the period the community has changed, and the school now draws a student population from all socio-economic levels with the largest percentage of students reflecting the industrial climate of the district. The administrators and teachers are generally a conservative lot and have had some difficulty accepting the behavior codes that have changed somewhat in the last decade. In short, many teachers are uncomfortable with the fact that students are less cooperative and seemingly less interested in school than was previously the case.

One morning during a discussion in the teacher's lounge, about student behavior, Mrs. Morgan commented that she was very pleased with the improvement of one of her students, Harry Davis. He was a large boy who had frequently been in trouble for intimidating younger and smaller students. Harry's apparent change caused Mrs. Morgan to be optimistic that he was maturing. Some of the other teachers who also knew him took a more skeptical approach, doubting that he was much different.

Not too long after that Mr. Walls, the principal, said it had been reported that students were smoking on the school grounds and he asked the teachers to monitor for any infringements of the school rules. During the lunch break, as Mr. Lopez, the Spanish teacher, was leaving the school premises, he observed that Harry

94

was smoking as he walked across the campus. He reported the incident to Mr. Walls who summarily suspended Harry for this violation. The boy denied that he was smoking and stated that he was being treated unfairly because the principal was accepting a teacher's report without question. He complained that it was unfair for a student to be suspended for smoking when teachers "do it all the time."

The next morning Harry returned to school with his parents. Mrs. Morgan and Mr. Lopez were called to the office to discuss the case with the principal and with the boy's parents.

### Becoming Involved

1. Did Mr. Lopez, the teacher, violate the rights of the student when he reported that he saw the boy smoking?

2. Was Harry correct in stating that he had as much right to smoke as the teachers?

3. Did the principal make an error in suspending Harry without further investigation of the accusation?

4. In what other way could the principal be criticized for his handling of the incident?

### Field Exploration

Talk with a principal or dean. Ask him what procedures he uses in suspending a student. Does he rely on teachers for evidence which warrants suspension?

### The Coalition for Student Rights

The Coalition for Student Rights is a group at Hamilton High led by five students who wish to transform the Student Council into a more powerful Student Senate. The group has continually pressed to get its demands accepted and the constant agitation has prompted much discussion and some argument at the school. The administration has officially ignored the group, but the demands were becoming so frequent that some response had to be made.

The principal and the dean of boys finally decided to take action. They suspended the five leaders on the grounds that their meetings were disrupting school activities, telling them not to return until they consented to discontinue their protests.

The students' parents have become involved. They asked directly and later through public media whether the purpose of the school is to educate or to dominate students. They are also demanding that the administrators reinstate their children with no penalties for days missed.

Meanwhile back at the school, a group of sympathetic demonstrators have gathered in the hall outside the principal's office. Several pupils are on their "soapboxes" trying to rally the students on the behalf of the expelled five. This situation is causing quite a disturbance.

Behavior in most classrooms is similar to that in the hallways. The patience of each teacher is wearing thin, yet each is doing his best to maintain a high standard of learning in his classes. Everyone knows that conditions between the school and community will worsen before they improve, and any improvement may be weeks away.

### Becoming Involved

1. On what grounds were the five students expelled?
2. What was the real reason for the expulsions?
3. Is the problem really any concern of the teachers or should it be limited to the principal, dean, and expelled students?
4. Should the teachers mention the problem in their classes?

### Field Exploration

Invite some members of a student council to come to a class meeting. Ask them to share with the class some of the "needed" rights which they are working toward and some of the privileges which they have recently been granted.

## Who Are You To Say?

It was Miss Adams' fate to begin her teaching experience by presenting a unit on Shakespeare's *Othello* to her college-bound students. Even though it is a difficult play for an inexperienced instructor, the group seemingly progressed very well. The instructional unit was completed in four weeks and she was pleased that the students were able to express definite, well-considered opinions in their discussions.

Miss Adams decided to devote the subsequent week to having the class write adaptations of *Othello* as if it were set in the present environment. On the day that the essays were due, each student was to share an oral summary of his paper with the class. Geoff and Evan shared creative ideas in their oral reports; however, when Miss Adams began to read the essays she discovered that their written statements were completely different. In reality, she felt that both of them had submitted nothing less than pornography.

She placed failing grades on the papers and then privately informed the boys that she was shocked that they used this project to demonstrate such gutteral language. When she asked for an apology, both boys angrily confronted her, complaining that she was trying to impose her standards of morality on them by giving them failing grades on the papers. They insisted that their parents would support them in demanding that they be given passing grades and that she had no right to moralize on their methods of expressing themslves.

Miss Adams was bewildered. Although she was inexperienced, she felt that she had the right to make such a judgment and was shocked at the boys' behavior. Grades were due in one week, so the final decision had to be made relatively soon.

### Becoming Involved

1. On what grounds did Miss Adams base her decision to require written and oral adaptations of the play?

2. What evidence was there that the boys were aware that their words would be interpreted as offensive?

3. Was Miss Adams partially responsible for the offensive papers?

## Field Exploration

Does the teacher have a right to try to persuade students to adopt certain morals? Those who answer yes assemble and appoint members to represent John and Bill. The remainder of the group will represent the boys' parents and friends.

Those students who answer no, select a member to represent Miss Adams. The others will represent those parents of the students who support Miss Adams.

Reenact the complete incident. When the role playing has been completed, make a list of responsibilities of teachers for providing moral leadership and a list of student rights which should not be violated.

## Billy the Punk

Bob Jennings began his preservice experiences in industrial education at the beginning of the second semester. While talking to a few teachers one day, the topic of conversation turned to a boy called "Billy the Punk." He was described as the school's main discipline problem and no one had a kind word for him. Subsequent conversations continued to focus on the rebellious student.

During his second week of teaching, Bob was assigned a new section of students in advanced woods. As he checked the roll, he noticed that the name Billy Punk, with the name "Wilson" in parentheses, was on the list. The class laughed when Billy's name was called and one student remarked that he had been expelled for a week because he had been involved in a scuffle. Bob discussed this matter with Mr. Peabody, his supervisor, and also inquired about the name "Wilson" in parentheses. Mr. Peabody explained that Punk was the boy's real name, but Wilson was the name that he preferred because his parents had deserted him as a child and an aunt and uncle named Wilson had given him a home. They had never adopted him.

Bob decided to refer to the boy by the name which he preferred and discovered that Billy was cooperative and did creditable work in his woods class. Bob observed some of Billy's other classes and noticed that the teachers and students treated him indifferently. In turn, he seemed withdrawn and unresponsive in those classes.

A few weeks later, Bob observed Mr. Myers, the high school principal, admonishing a student for running in the halls. Billy, who was standing nearby burst into laughter. Mr. Myers approached Billy, grabbed him by the arms and jostled him to the wall of the corridor. Mr. Myers noticed that Bob had observed the incident and explained that Billy was worthless and should be removed from school because he was constantly in trouble.

During the next week, Billy submitted his project for grading It was a beautiful desk set, and the boy seemed proud of his accomplishment. He certainly had not displayed any of his hostile behaviors in this class.

On the Wednesday prior to the completion of his preservice experience, Bob discovered that Billy had been in a fight at the basketball game and injured a hand when he hit an object. When he entered the teachers' lounge during the lunch break, he was not at all surprised to see that the conversation focused on the scuffle at the game. All seemed to agree that Billy had caused the fight. Speculation ran high about whether or not he would now be permanently suspended from school.

### Becoming Involved

1. On the surface, it appears that Billy is just a troubled youth who is having difficulty coping with school. On closer observation, however, can you discover some fundamental principles which should be of concern to teachers who teach such students?

2. What can Billy's teachers do to help him?

3. How do you analyze the term, "worthless student," as it relates to Billy?

4. Should Mr. Myers have physically confronted Billy?

## Field Exploration

Students today are searching and fighting to maintain their identity. What legal rights do students have in this plight? Can a student change his name and, if so, must a teacher accept and respect this change? What other personal rights must teachers respect?

See if you can contact an expert in school law (a professor on campus or a representative of the local education association are possibilities). Ask him to speak to your group concerning the emerging legal rights of students.

## Jim's Interpretation

The assigned short story for the particular day was one that contained a few four-letter words. They were not actually abusive expressions, but as the discussion proceeded it became apparent that some of the girls in class were offended and embarrassed by what they had read. Miss Pittinger realized that there were numerous religious students in her classroom; yet she failed to anticipate the feelings of animosity which later developed toward the short story. In order to prove the significance of the coarse words to her puzzled students, she decided to ask different ones to read passages aloud. There were no volunteers, so she unthinkingly called on Jim, who had always been somewhat of an enigma.

Jim began reading smoothly; however, whenever a word such as "damn" or "hell" appeared, he would place excessive emphasis on these words. This dramatic reading visibly upset several of the girls. Finally Miss Pittinger felt it necessary to stop the activity in partial aggravation at Jim and at the innocence of her students. Jim looked up at her, smiled, and halted at her command.

Miss Pittinger felt uneasy as it became apparent that she would have to explain how these "four letter words" were used to enable the author to portray his style. By this time, several students were completely ignoring her, and she seemed to be groping for an explanation to justify the author's technique. Finally Shirley flatly stated that she was disgusted with the teacher, the short story, and most of all, with Jim's interpretation.

Jim was obviously provoked, and Miss Pittinger waited to hear his retort. He noticed her frozen condition and launched into a defense of his reading. He called the disturbed students religious freaks, using a variety of four-letter words in his accusation. Miss Pittinger ordered him to stop, realizing in turn, that he might accuse her of being hypocritical.

Jim stood up, turned to Miss Pittinger, uttered an epithet and stormed out of the room with a curse on his lips that embarrassed and stunned the liberal Miss Pittinger. He left her with one final idea. "After all, if the authors have the right to use four-letter words in the textbooks shouldn't students have the same privilege?"

### Becoming Involved

1. Apart from assigning this short story for homework, what was Miss Pittinger's first mistake?

2. Suggest a more acceptable approach which Miss Pittinger might use to achieve her purpose.

3. Is a teacher wrong for imposing four-letter words on students?

### Field Exploration

Contact various people in the community (ministers, parents, and American Civil Liberties Union members are logical possibilities) and solicit their views in regard to profanity. Should it be contained in textbooks? Should teachers attempt to control the use of four-letter words at school?

### WHAT THE EXPERTS SAY

Teachers have always seemed to feel that students are becoming more independent and more difficult to manage. This concern, once lightly regarded, has suddenly acquired new meaning. Students are now beginning to seriously exercise their demands for rights and are finding that courts are generally favorable to their complaints, pointing out that due process and civil liberties have been denied.

A study of high school students[1] sought to acquire their perceptions of teacher violations of human rights. The data revealed that 81 percent of those questioned perceived their most violated right to be teacher respect for student opinion. Other violations as perceived by students were denial of rights of association, while seniors manifested particular concern regarding administrative censorship of student activities.

Most of the action concerning student rights, however, is happening in the nation's courts. According to a recent publication on student rights, "The once traditional reluctance of the courts to exercise their power in the educational sphere is fast becoming a thing of the past."[2] The United States Supreme Court decision in the Tinker vs. Des Moines Community School District[3] is the landmark decision in this area. The most popular phrase stated, "First Amendment rights, applied in light of the special characteristic of the school environment, are available to teachers and students. It can hardly be argued that either students or teachers shed their constitutional rights to freedom of speech or expression at the schoolhouse gate."

The guidelines handed down by the federal district court in the Northern District of California in the case of Towe vs. Campbell Union High School District[4] may be considered to be an interpretation of some of the new relationships which will need to be practiced in the schools:

1. Students are "persons" within the meaning of the Constitution and are possessed of fundamental rights which are not lost in school.

[1]Thomas H. Buxron and Keith W. Prichard, "Student Perceptions of Teacher Violations of Human Rights," *Phi Delta Kappan* 50:1, Sept., 1973, pp. 66-9.

[2]Martin, Haberman, *Students' Rights; A Guide to the Rights of Children, Youth, and Future Teachers,* Assoc. of Teacher Educators Bulletin No. 34, ATE, Washington, D.C., August, 1973, pp. 2.

[3]Tinker vs. Des Moines Independent Community School District, 393 U.S. 503 1969.

[4]*Op Cit.,* pp. 6-7.

2. Students are not the "closed circuit" recipients of only that which the state wishes to communicate: they may not be confined to official approved sentiments.

3. Student freedom of speech includes personal inter-communication of controversial ideas.

4. School officials have the burden of showing constitutionally valid justifications for limitations on student speech.

5. A generalized fear or apprehension of a disturbance is not a constitutionally adequate justification. A desire to avoid the expression of controversial or unpopular ideas or the discomfort and unpleasantness which accompany them is not a constitutionally adequate justification.

6. School officials must demonstrate that the prohibited speech would have **actually caused** substantial and material disruption of, or interference with, classwork, or with the requirements of discipline appropriate to the operation of the school.

The fundamental legal concept regarding student rights is the notion that students are as entitled to the same protection afforded by the Constitution as their elders. It is the constitutional right of every American to be assumed innocent of charges against him until proven otherwise in a fair and open hearing. Presumably, this applies equally to students and adults. Both are entitled to due process, which includes the rights to prior notice, formal charges, representation by counsel, cross-examination of witnesses and appeal of adverse decisions.

Two recent Supreme Court decisions[5] have supported the concept of student rights. In Goss v. Lopez, it ruled that a student may not be suspended without a hearing of some sort, however informal. If a student is suspended, he must be informed of the reasons for suspension.

School board members may be sued for damages by a student if they act officially in violation of the student's constitutional rights or with malicious intent to injure him, according to the Court's decision in Wood vs. Strickland--informally known as the "Spiked Punch Case."

[5]Quoted from *Phi Delta Kappan*, LVI No. 8 Apr. 1975, p. 574.

Many feel that the Court has guaranteed all constitutional rights to students in the public schools. However, by including the phrase, "in the light of special characteristics of the school environment," in the Tinker case, others feel that those rights in the schools are somewhat different from constitutional rights guaranteed in the larger society. This problem of discriminating between the two will probably be the basis for further action during the next few years.

Teachers will be faced with decisions in areas ranging from freedom of speech to the modification of pupil behavior which is considered to be unsatisfactory. Although some may be wringing their hands wondering how to control children, the true professional should consider this new set of circumstances to be a challenge to teach in such a way that students will respond positively without confrontation. Instead of relying on coercion, teachers may have to be more persuasive. Trust will sometimes have to replace suspicion, and students may have to be treated as people who can accept responsibility rather than as children who need to have every movement controlled.

The advent of student rights may actually initiate a more mature school environment and bridge the gap between student and teacher as the students become more aware of their rights and accompanying responsibilities. Self-discipline may very well replace imposed discipline as teachers and students come to view each other differently.

## DISCUSSION OF QUESTIONS

### Innocent Until Proven Guilty

1. *Did Mr. Lopez, the teacher, violate the rights of the student when he reported that he saw the boy smoking?* No. He merely reported his observation as he was instructed to do. If he had not reported the incident, he might have violated more student rights, in that he would have ignored a rule which was established to protect students.

2. *Was Harry correct in stating that he had as much right to smoke as the teachers?* Some believe that he may be, although his weakness was the failure to observe that teachers are usually permitted to smoke only in designated sections of the school campus. Harry's case would have been stronger if he had complained that students have no designated smoking area.

3. *Did the principal make an error in suspending Harry without further investigation of the accusation?* If he made an error, it was not because of his lack of investigation, but because of the fact that he did not exercise due process, i.e., informing the student of the reason for suspension and giving him an opportunity to present a defense, to be confronted directly with the evidence against him, and even to having counsel of some sort if he so desired.

4. *In what other way could the principal be criticized for his handling of the incident?* He precipitously dismissed the student in spite of the fact that his behavior was reported to have been improving by at least one teacher. It may appear that he is deliberately attempting to suspend the boy instead of recognizing that he is making some improvement in behavior.

### The Coalition for Student Rights

1. *On what grounds were the five students expelled?* The basis given for expulsion was because they were disrupting school activities.

2. *What was the real reason for the expulsions?* The leadership of the five was threatening to the administration. The "meetings" issue was used to curtail the student activities.

3. *Is the problem really any concern of the teachers or should it be limited to the principal, dean and expelled students?* The real problem is an issue for teacher concern, for now it has reached the level of disrupting school activities.

4. *Should the teachers mention the problem in their classes?* Since the basic need of malcontents is a way to express themselves, the classroom seems an appropriate place to voice their grievances.

### Who Are You To Say

1. *On what grounds did Miss Adams base her decision to require written and oral adaptations of the play?* Her decision to permit the students to do written and oral adaptations of the play was an attempt to provide more responsibility and to permit them to express themselves creatively.

2. *What evidence was there that the boys were aware that their words would be interpreted as offensive?* The boys' oral presentations were different from their written presentations. Apparently they had been reluctant to use the offensive words in their spoken reports.

3. *Was Miss Adams partially responsible for the offensive papers?* Although Miss Adams cannot be held responsible for the boys' vulgarity, she should explain why it is inappropriate in either oral or written reports.

### Billy the Punk

1. *On the surface, it appears that Billy is just a troubled youth who is having difficulty coping with school. On closer observation, however, can you discover some fundamental principles which should be of concern to teachers who teach such students?* It appears that an analysis of human rights is involved.

Teachers should respect the desire of students in regard to names, for example. In a broader context, too, the nature of freedom of expression should be examined as it relates to Billy.

2. *What can Billy's teachers do to help him?* They can treat him with respect, as he apparently responds favorably when a teacher takes the time to do so. They can also help him to understand that a student may find more acceptable ways to problem solving than fighting. Rights are **submerged** when force has to be employed.

3. *How do you analyze the term, "worthless **student**," as it relates to Billy?* It seems to be a generality which characterizes the boy. It may be ill-conceived in that some of the evidence indicates that he has respect for those who really care for him.

4. *Should Mr. Myers have physically confronted Billy?* No, an educator is in a position of leadership, and he should refrain from engaging in physical confrontations because they symbolize a collapse of reason. Of more pragmatic concern is the fact that he may be held liable for legal redress.

### Jim's Interpretation

1. *Apart from assigning this short story for homework, what was Miss Pittinger's first mistake?* Her lack of respect for the students when she perceived they were uncomfortable with the kind of language used in the story.

2. *Suggest a more acceptable approach which Miss Pittinger might use to achieve her purpose.* She could first alert the students to the contents of the assignment and explain the purpose of such an activity. Then, according to their reactions, she could decide whether she should or should not read the composition in class.

3. *Is a teacher wrong for imposing four-letter words on students?* Since it is generally questionable for a teacher to impose his values or beliefs upon students, it logically follows that this action would be inappropriate. However, one would assume that the teacher's intent in this case was not to impose but to simply acquaint students with a writer's style. The imposition came through an error in judgment.

107

### POST-ASSESSMENT

| | A G R E E | D I S A G R E E | U N D E C I D E D |
|---|---|---|---|

*How do you feel?*

1. If students receive too many rights, there will be constant problems for the school. — — —

2. Students should not have the same prerogatives as adults because they are not mature enough to accept the accompanying responsibilities. — — —

3. When making decisions regarding student privileges, the teacher should give more consideration to the pupil's previous record than his "rights." — — —

4. Teacher rights should receive priority over student demands. — — —

5. Too many student rights have been granted too suddenly. — — —

*What do you think?*

1. The individual liberties of citizens are not guaranteed to students who are under eighteen because, like a guardian, the school is responsible for their welfare. — — —

2. In case of suspension, the student has the right to be confronted with the evidence against him. — — —

3. A right in the broadest sense is more than a legal term. — — —

4. Students are now able to successfully contest teachers' decisions. — — —

5. Group rights supersede individual preferences in the classroom. — — —

## SELF-ASSESSMENT

Now that you have completed the post-assessment, compare your pre- and post- test scores. Check those items where there is disagreement between responses. Examine your reasons for any changes in your responses; when possible, cite the specific reasons which had some influence on that change.

1. To what degree, if any, are teachers responsible for helping students secure their rights?

2. Some students are unrealistic about what rights they think they are due. Should teachers help these students realize when their expectations are unrealistic?

3. When students fight for rights which conflict with the educational goals of the institution, should the teacher oppose those students?

4. When should students be involved in the decision making at schools and when should they not?

5. Will there be significant changes in the schools as a result of the student rights movement?

## FURTHER INVOLVEMENT

BETCHKAL, JAMES, Editor, "Children's Rights: the Mounting Issue Over Which School Leaders Next Must Agonize," *American School Board Journal* 160:41-42, March, 1973.

This article first disarms you with some amusing anecdotes about pupil behavior and then levels a broadside when it submits that public school authorities routinely violate the constitutional rights of children more than any other branch of government. It then attempts to explain why. You may or may not agree with it, but it will make you think and probably get you into a debate with someone else in class.

CLAYTON, EDWARD M., and JACOBSEN, GENE, "An Analysis of Court Cases Concerned with Students Rights 1960-1971," *NASSP Bulletin* 58:49-53, February, 1974.

A brief summary of court decisions in such areas as suspension and expulsion, student publication, school attendance, and search of locker and purses. It concludes with nine recommendations which should create a sensible educational atmosphere and still be within court guidelines.

FLYGARE, THOMAS J., *The Legal Rights of Students*, Phi Delta Kappa, Bloomington, IN., 1975.

The author, who is an attorney and a former secondary teacher, discusses issues such as discrimination, student records, student searches, religion, freedom of speech, publication and distribution of literature, suspensions, expulsions, and dress codes.

JACOB, GEORGE F., and RICHTER, JAMES P., "Student Rights Require a Model for Change," *NASSP Bulletin* 58: 41-8, February 1974.

Describes a procedure to protect student rights and improve the process of identifying students' social, emotional, or learning problems which presents an alternative to expulsion of students.

MANDEL, RICHARD, "Judicial Decisions and Organizational Change in Public Schools," *School Review* 82:327-46, February, 1974.

A lawyer examines the effect of judicial process upon the schools. Comments include regulating student activity, procedures for punishing students, student rights, and religion. It closes with a discussion of the question, "Can the courts change schools?" If you want to impress your friends (and your professor) read this one.

NATIONAL EDUCATION ASSOCIATION, "Let's Set the Record Straight on Student Rights," *Today's Education* 64:3, September-October, 1975, pp. 69--70.

Interprets the Goss v. Lopez case, indicating what the decision means for teachers.

NOLTE, CHESTER, "Brush Up In One Short Sitting; Ten Years of Tumult in School Law, and Their Lessons," *American School Board Journal* 161:48-51.

The author reviews the last ten years and submits that it has brought drastic changes to the operation of schools. He examines briefly some of the significant changes that have taken place. A good way to get a quick look at what has happened in the courts as it reflects on education.

*PHI DELTA KAPPA*, December, 1974. *Phi Delta Kappan* 8th and Union, Bloomington, Indiana, 47401.

The entire issue is devoted to the changing concept of student rights. The topic is approached from several divergent viewpoints including a model code of student rights. Don't miss the "Letter from an Angry Teacher" on the back cover.

## Chapter Six

## ASSESSING PUPIL PROGRESS

|  | AGREE | DISAGREE | UNDECIDED |
|---|---|---|---|

### PRE-ASSESSMENT

*How do you feel?*

1. While some students may work for grades, most seek more from school than bringing home good marks. — — —

2. Out-of-school factors are more important than classroom instruction in determining pupil growth. — — —

3. A student who is working to his potential should pass regardless of the quality of his work. — — —

4. A teacher should resist those outside pressures intended to affect his assessment of his students' performance. — — —

5. A teacher should change a grade only when he is certain that he has made a computational or recording error. — — —

*What do you think?*

1. Grading is a rather simple and enjoyable task for most teachers. — — —

2. A student can easily be motivated by the threat of a reduced or failing grade. — — —

3. A student who talks with another student during a test is probably cheating. — — —

4. Successful teaching is evidenced by better grades. — — —

5. The major purpose of a test is to evaluate students. — — —

111

## INTRODUCTION

As a student preparing for an examination, how many times have you remarked or thought, "If only I could be giving this exam rather than taking it"? Now that you realize you are eventualiy going to assume that role, are you still eager to be an evaluator? Most teachers do not derive excessive pleasure from this task. In fact, grading is often thought of as an unpleasant responsibility that cannot be avoided.

Many contemporary· educators insist that far too much emphasis is placed on the evaluation process. Be that as it may, grading is perhaps the most common area of conflict between teachers and parents and between students and teachers. Although many college professors, college students, and teachers insist that stress on the importance of grades makes learning superficial, the practice continues. Many people, including educators, parents, and students insist that grades provide motivation and a basis for comparing performance with other students.

Although the purposes of grading may become distorted and confused, there are some very important reasons for this type of assessment. When correctly utilized, grading provides feedback to the teacher and to the recipients. The student can have a basis for comparing his performance with that of his peers or he can compare his current progress with his achievement during a previous period. Testing can be used to diagnose student weaknesses or teaching deficiencies. When properly used, an evaluation can help pinpoint areas of confusion and misunderstanding, and it can provide motivation to students.

Whether grading will be a process for students to fear and teachers to despise or whether it will be a procedure which offers helpful feedback to both pupil and instructor will depend largely upon the teacher's approach to evaluation. The experiences in this section have been selected because they provide examples of how teachers must make decisions in assessing pupil progress. Were you that teacher, how would you avoid or cope with the situation? For when you get your own classes, your decisions will determine whether grading will be an ominous liability or a significant asset.

## IN THE CLASSROOM

### The Star Player Failed

Athletics play an important part in the lives of the residents of Elizabeth City. Basketball is the major sport, and during every home game the gymnasium is packed with fans who have come to watch the team play (and win).

Eric Snow was a second-year teacher at El High who was considered by the faculty, parents, and students to be an outstanding math teacher in a department which had an excellent reputation for scholarship. Tom Winston, a student in the senior math class, was a member of the varsity basketball squad. Over the past five years, his father, a man of means, had obviously secured influence over the school board.

Mr. Snow had observed that Tom was doing very poorly in this math class in spite of his apparent capability to do better. He was concerned about Tom's grades since the semester was drawing to an end and he did not want to issue him a failing mark. He offered to help Tom with any problems but all offers were rejected.

At the end of the grading period, Eric felt that he had no other choice but to record a failing grade for Tom. When the student received the report, he was furious. He knew he had to have a higher grade to play ball and it was important to his father that he participate in the biggest game of the year.

Tom went to Mr. Snow and demanded a grade change. Mr. Snow explained that he could not do so, citing the fact that he had offered his assistance on a number of occasions and was refused. Tom angrily announced that his father had a way of convincing people to change their minds.

### *Becoming Involved*

1. Cite an exact instance in which Mr. Snow's behavior reflected true professionalism.

2. What effect might a change in grade have on Tom?

113

3. What effect might a change in Tom's grade have on other students?

### Field Exploration

What procedures are used by teachers to alert students to the fact that their work is not meeting minimum standards? Talk with a few teachers and compile a list of practices. Do they support or refute the procedures used by Mr. Snow?

## "I Just Knew He Had Copied"

Dan is an above-average student who is an independent thinker. He was confounded when his English teacher returned a homework theme which contained the accusation that it had been copied from another student's work.

Dan sought help from his counselor, who advised him that the best and quickest solution would be to sit down for a few minutes and write another theme to satisfy the teacher. Dan felt that this suggestion was absurd since it would be an admission of guilt.

The counselor sent for Dan the following week and told him both he and the teacher could testify, giving their sides of the conflict. When Dan presented his defense, he asked the teacher to display the theme which he had been accused of copying. The teacher said that she could not produce it, but she "just knew he had copied." She did not have the theme or any concrete evidence of any kind, but she stated that she had read that work before. The counselor and teacher both felt that Dan should admit his lack of integrity since it was the English teacher's class and her prerogative to accept and reject pupil work.

### Becoming Involved

1. What important factors does this teacher appear to ignore?
2. There must have been some basis for the teacher's positive feelings about Dan's cheating. What are some possibilities?
3. One alternative for this teacher would be to have remained

114

quiet and set a trap for Dan. Do you feel that the teacher would be justified in doing this?

4. Instead of accusing Dan of copying, what other alternatives could the teacher have considered?

### Field Exploration

Some teachers seem to be able to intuitively know when a student cheats. Ask a teacher how he detects deception in his classes and what he does once it is suspected or discovered. Then talk to a few students. Ask them if they have felt they have been unjustly accused of cheating. How do they feel about the teacher who made the accusation?

## The Old Pop Quiz

Ms. Barnet, a new student teacher, wanted to get the students to read the textbook. She concluded that a pop quiz would be successful in achieving that objective, so she told the students on Monday to read chapter six in the text before the week was over.

Friday, when Ms. Barnet entered the classroom, she asked the students to close the books and take out pencils; then she administered an oral quiz. The results were disastrous. Only one of fifteen students received a passing grade. Ms. Barnet had not been prepared for this and assumed that the students were failing to exert any effort.

She took the results to her supervisor and asked what she should do about it. He smiled and stated that secondary students must be closely monitored. He informed her that a teacher must first present or discuss the material before a test is given. Since the supervising teacher would be evaluating her, she complied without protest. However, she felt that this procedure would not encourage the pupils to read.

### Becoming Involved

1. What was Ms. Barnet's mistake which started her problem?
2. What faulty assumption did Ms. Barnet make about the students?

3. Should pop quizzes be used as motivation techniques?

4. What would you advise her to do to prevent future testing problems?

### *Field Exploration*

If you have the opportunity to work with a group of students for several days, administer an unannounced quiz. How did the students react to it? Was their performance as satisfactory as you had anticipated?

If this is not feasible, ask a teacher if you can score a set of quiz papers. What is the range of scores? Are there any surprises?

### Mr. Smith's Problem

Lyle Smith, an impressive new teacher, was selected from a long list of candidates to teach at Mallard High School. The first nine weeks passed uneventfully. As the second grading period ended, though, he became very concerned about Kim, who seemingly had changed personalities since school began. The cooperative, interested student had become lethargic and indifferent. She ceased participating in class and often laid her head down and slept through the discussion. Her grade was plummeting and she had sometimes seemed insolent and defiant.

Mr. Smith decided to explore the reasons for the change in this student. He learned that Kim was intelligent and capable of obtaining above average grades, but that her performance had also deteriorated in other classes. The counselor informed him that Kim's mother had initiated proceedings for dissolution of marriage against her father.

After the investigation, Mr. Smith had no doubts as to why Kim was performing below her ability. He decided to talk with her, but she failed to show up at the designated hour. Her only response the next day was that she was busy and did not want any help. With that she became silent and refused to discuss the matter further.

As the grading period drew to a close, Kim's grades and attitude had not improved. In fact, her last quiz was returned without a single question answered. As the deadline for grade reports approached, Mr. Smith was really concerned about this situation. He knew some reasons for her behavior, but could not understand why she refused help. He also wondered whether he should become involved in this personal matter. The ultimate question was whether he should give a lower grade to a girl who was having difficulty in school due to personal problems at home. He spent an uncomfortable afternoon before submitting his final grade report.

### Becoming Involved

1. What was the apparent reason for Kim's falling into this pattern of behavior?

2. Should Mr. Smith have singled out Kim and offered to help her?

3. If you were the teacher, what grade would you give Kim? Why?

4. How could Mr. Smith help Kim through this difficult period?

### Field Exploration

What do the teachers do when they see that a student is not performing as well as previously? Talk with teachers about students who suddenly make lower grades. What do they do in attempting to help the student?

## Two Points May Change a Life

The last week of the grading period had arrived. Miss Lane had planned to climax her unit in physical education with a proficiency test and a written examination. She had decided to grade on attitude, participation, skills, and the written test. Becky, her most baffling student, was better than average on the proficiency test but she failed the written component by a significant margin. According to the cumulative score, Becky's total grade points added

117

to a total of sixty-three out of a possible one hundred points—two points below the passing score.

Should she change her grading scale two points so that the girl would pass? Becky had displayed a negative attitude about school in general and physical education in particular. She rudely challenged Miss Lane and seemed to be unpopular with the other students.

Becky had once improved briefly after Miss Lane conferred with her, but she soon regressed to her former style. She insisted on addressing her teacher as "Lane", and she frequently yelled and screamed at the other students. Miss Lane threatened detention, but Becky shrugged it off by saying that she had to leave immediately after school in order to care for her younger brother and sister. Upon investigation, Miss Lane found that this statement was true.

The parents were reported to be unconcerned about her school work and often sent notes so she could be excused from classes. It appeared that Becky's symptoms were the result of personal problems rather than of direct animosity toward the teacher.

Miss Lane glanced at her grade book again and was still confronted with the two-point discrepancy. If Becky failed she would have to repeat physical education next year and would probably be even less enchanted with school. If she were awarded the two points needed to pass would she expect and depend upon similar gifts in the future?

### Becoming Involved

1. Was Becky's failure due to the quality of the test?
2. Becky was not really exerting any effort to pass, yet she was only two points below a passing grade. Which of these factors is more important in deciding whether or not she should pass?
3. Part of the point total was a subjective appraisal of attitude. Is this justifiable?

### Field Exploration

Prepare a set of factors which you would use for making subjective evaluations of pupils in your teaching field. First, discuss them in class and then revise them. Then, present your criteria to a practicing teacher and ask him to comment. Perhaps there may be an occasional situation where you could actually implement your system and observe its effectiveness.

### Don't Talk During the Test

After about a week and a half of teaching, Maria decided that it was time for the first test. Since this was the first exam that she had prepared and administered, she was excited about the possibilities. However she found herself ill prepared for the difficulties of administration due to an unexpected complication.

Maria distributed papers face down on the desks. She carefully explained the instructions and gave a specific reminder that any talking would be considered an act of cheating and treated accordingly. She also stated that when the students were finished, they could turn in their papers and begin preparing for tomorrow's assignment. About mid-way through the class period, she observed that two girls in the back row, Cheryl and Rhea, were talking.

Maria considered the proper course of action and then decided to ask how many individuals were still working on the quiz. Cheryl raised her hand when the question was presented to the group. Rhea did not because she had already completed the test. When Cheryl brought her paper to the desk, the teacher informed her that she had violated the talking rule that she had given at the beginning of the exercise. Cheryl was upset and emphatically denied that she had cheated. She asked Maria what she was going to do.

What should she do?

### *Becoming Involved*

1. What are the implications if the teacher gives each of the girls a failing grade?

2. What is one of the fundamental questions which must be considered before a decision is made?

3. Should teachers have the right to fail students if they talk during a test?

### Field Exploration

A teacher cannot take a casual attitude toward test administration and expect a minimum of problems. Talk with a few experienced teachers concerning the techniques which they have found helpful in seeing that a test is fairly administered. How do they prevent talking during a test, and what course of action do they take if they observe two people in conversation? Do they rely heavily on absolute rules?

## WHAT THE EXPERTS SAY

The area of assessing pupil progress is a very complex one which requires extensive study before it can be completely understood. It ranges from simple quiz formulation through consideration of criteria which constitute a grade.

A teaching candidate may find himself immediately thrust into the position of having to cope with problems related to evaluation. If the previous case studies are typical, they indicated that the use of tests as motivating devices seems to be of prime concern. How many times have you heard a teacher threaten to use a quiz to force completion of an assignment or to motivate or discipline a student? How valid is the assumption that students fear low grades and will, hence, follow a teacher's bidding if they are threatened with poor scores?

Many educators see grades as motivating devices, but research suggests that when tests are used in the traditional manner the downgraded students continue to fail.[1] Since very few students are encouraged (or rewarded) for going back to review material which they do not know, there is usually little effort to review or to build the skills that have not been learned. Thus, failure is often compounded.

The threat of a quiz or test is often purported to be a guaranteed method of forcing students to perform. Yet frustrated teachers often note that a threat is often ignored. Why? A study of the effect of anxiety upon grades indicated that anxiety lowered the grades of middle-ability students while anxiety producing

[1]Normal M. Chansky, "The X-Ray of the School Mark," *The Educational Forum*, March, 1962, pp. 347-52.

conditions actually increased the grades of high ability students.[2] It could be concluded that when tests are used to force students to perform, those who are to be motivated by the procedure are the ones least likely to succeed.

Many teachers share the concern of Miss Lane (Two Points May Change a Life) and feel that increased leniency in marking over a period of time will cause students to quit devoting any effort to study. But a research study of two equal groups who were given differing grades[3] found that the mark given did not have any consistent influence on the variables measured--motivation, learning comprehension, speaking, short quizzes, homework, or the final examination. The results of this study suggest that many of the arguments on the effects of marking |may be grossly over-stated. Over a one-semester period, the relative level of marking seemed to have little impact on motivation or achievement for most students.

The experts seem to suggest that grades alone, or threats of tests or lower grades, do not achieve increased learning. The purposes of testing and evaluation should be the improvement of instruction rather than coercion to conform. One expert insists that "the single most important use of evaluation in education is in adapting instruction to differing pupils' needs."[4]

Many cries are heard today to abolish all grading. In fact, many schools and school systems have consented to "non-graded" programs eliminating a need for tests. How effective are these programs? According to one person, "the various no-grade evaluation options recently introduced on the academic scene are grading in disguise."[5] This bit of information should cause teachers to look more carefully at the evaluation system to see if it is merely grading classified under some other rubric.

[2]Beeman Phillips, "Sex, Social Class and Anxiety as Sources of Variation in School Activity," *Journal of Educational Psychology*, 1962, 53:316-62.

[3]Jon C. Marshall and Diana L. Christensen, "Leniency in Marking: Its Effects on Student Motivation and Achievement," *Education* 93:3, February, 1973, pp. 262-265.

[4]Robert Murray, "Evaluation: The Educational Phenomenon," *Man/Society/Technology* 33:5, February, 1974, pp. 139-141.

[5]Henry Moulds, "To Grade or Not to Grade: A Futile Question," *Intellect* 102:2358, Summer, 1974, pp. 501-4.

The harm caused by grades results from competition rather than from the marks themselves, which only reflect the degree of damage. Many individualized programs attempt to minimize this problem by removing rivalry among students, so that each individual competes only with himself. Such programs usually involve the student in assessing his progress, providing immediate and continuous feedback which should motivate learning. One current educator not only implies that testing has the ability to promote learning, but even discusses a multiplicity of ways that testing can achieve this goal.[6]

According to Bloom, regardless of what type of evaluation is used, peer input is very important in terms of the course objectives.[7] Students should be involved in setting objectives and in the selection of tests to measure for the attainment of those objectives.

The experts present some of the prevailing thought and information on the topic. However, this is only a glance at a broad area and assessing pupil progress is a complicated process. Any serious teacher candidate should plan to devote considerable time and study of the process of evaluating student performance.

## DISCUSSION OF QUESTIONS

### The Star Player Failed

1. *Cite an exact instance in which Mr. Snow's behavior reflected true professionalism.* He extended an opportunity to help Tom to raise his failing grade. He then proceeded to treat him as he would other students.

2. *What effect might a change in grade have on Tom?* If Mr. Snow did change Tom's grade, his procrastination and threat to use power would be rewarded and therefore encouraged.

3. *What effect might a change in Tom's grade have on other students?* Somehow the word travels fast among peers. If Tom's

---

[6]Bert L. Kaplan, "Must Tests Be a Trial?" *Teacher* 91:5, January, 1974, pp. 20-2.
[7]Thomas K. Bloom, "Peer Evaluation: A Strategy for Student Involvement." *Man/Society/Technology*, 33:5, Feb., 1974, pp. 137-8.

threats were successful, his friends would be encouraged to emulate his behavior. Other students would probably resent Mr. Snow for being weak and showing partiality toward Tom.

## I Just Knew He Had Copied

1. *What important factors does this teacher appear to ignore?* Her memory may have been faulty, and there was no concrete proof that he had copied.

2. *There must have been some basis for the teacher's positive feelings about Dan's cheating. What are some possibilities?* The teacher may have observed some condition which caused her to feel that the work was not original. Also, the quality of the work might have been superior to his other creations. Obviously, the teacher was also relying somewhat on intuition or memory as indicated by the statement that she had previously read a similar paper.

3. *One alternative for this teacher would be to have remained quiet and set a trap for Dan. Do you feel that the teacher would be justified in doing this?* It is unethical for a teacher to set a trap for any student, for by doing so he might encourage Dan or other students to cheat.

4. *Instead of accusing Dan of copying, what other alternatives could the teacher have considered?* She might have questioned him extensively to test the boy's knowledge, or she could have sought evidence to support her contention.

## The Old Pop Quiz

1. *What was Ms. Barnet's mistake which started her problem?* She depended on a pop quiz to stimulate the students.

2. *What faulty assumption did Ms. Barnet make about the students?* She assumed that they would read and understand the vague homework assignment.

3. *Should pop quizzes be used as motivation techniques?* Tests, exams, and quizzes should be given unannounced only when they can be administered without creating fear and hostility

among students. When an instrument is used to "check-up" on the progress of a class, it should not be referred to as a test, quiz, or exam. To do so is to demean the proper purpose of tests. A better alternative would be to refer to it as an exercise, task, or practice problem.

4. *What would you advise her to do to prevent future testing problems?* To avoid similar future problems Ms. Barnet should be much more specific on her assignments by telling students what to look for. She should also apprise them of the fact that she would occasionally give unannounced quizzes.

### Mr. Smith's Problem

1. *What was the apparent reason for Kim's falling into this pattern of behavior?* She apparently was rebelling because her parents were involved in divorce procedures.

2. *Should Mr. Smith have singled out Kim and offered to help her?* Yes. His offer to meet with Kim demonstrated a concern and willingness to help.

3. *If you were the teacher, what grade would you give Kim? Why?* Kim should receive the grade which she earned. However, if and when she returns to her normal behavior you might extend her the opportunity to improve that grade.

4. *How could Mr. Smith help Kim through this difficult period?* At this time any gestures to help may be very limited. He could continue to express empathy and meanwhile discuss the problem with the school counselor who might provide some insights.

### Two Points May Change a Life

1. *Was Becky's failure due to the quality of the test?* We have no evidence to suggest that this is true. However, we do have evidence that Becky's poor showing is due partially to her negative attitude toward school.

2. *Becky was not really exerting any effort to pass yet she was only two points below a passing grade. Which of these factors is*

124

*more important in deciding whether or not she should pass?* The nearness of Becky's score to the passing mark is not as important as her attitude and her lack of initiative in the class.

3. *Part of the point total was a subjective appraisal of attitude. Is this justifiable?* Teachers often are bothered when a student receives a failing mark, as perhaps they should be. Yet, the normal reaction seems to be to search for a way in which they might be responsible for the student's failing. When subjective judgment has been used to determine a portion of the grade, the teacher often feels guilty for the failure. He should not feel this way at all especially if he combines his judgments with objective tests to reach his decision. His ability to make subjective judgments should be as good as his ability to select the right questions for tests.

### Don't Talk During the Test

1. *What are the implications if the teacher gives each of the girls a failing grade?* They may feel that the penalty was extreme and even if they had been sharing answers, a lesser penalty would have been more readily accepted.

2. *What is one of the fundamental questions which must be considered before a decision is made?* What type of response will most likely cause an improvement in future behavior?

3. *Should teachers have the right to fail students if they talk during a test?* Such an act seems to imply a state of desperation which will only lead to friction and alienation. An alternative which would enable the offending students to recover with less penalty may lead to more effective learning and a better classroom climate.

## POST-ASSESSMENT

| | AGREE | DISAGREE | UNDECIDED |
|---|---|---|---|

### How do you feel?

1. While some students may work for grades, most seek more from school than bringing home good marks. — — —

2. Out-of-school factors are more important than classroom instruction in determining pupil growth. — — —

3. A student who is working to his potential should pass regardless of the quality of his work. — — —

4. A teacher should resist those outside pressures intended to affect his assessment of his students' performance. — — —

5. A teacher should change a grade only when he is certain that he has made a computational or recording error. — — —

### What do you think?

1. Grading is a rather simple and enjoyable task for most teachers. — — —

2. A student can easily be motivated by the threat of a reduced or failing grade. — — —

3. A student who talks with another student during a test is probably cheating. — — —

4. Successful teaching is evidenced by better grades. — — —

5. The major purpose of a test is to evaluate students. — — —

126

## SELF-ASSESSMENT

Now that you have completed the post-assessment, compare your pre- and post-assessment scores. Check those questions for which there is disagreement between responses. Examine your reasons for change. When possible, cite the specific reason which influenced your change of opinion.

1. What are the purposes of tests?

2. What criteria must be established in determining a grade?

3. How can the teacher cope with his feelings toward students as he attempts to objectively determine a grade?

4. How much consideration should be given to the influence of out-of-class factors upon classroom performance?

5. Do lower grades provide more effective motivation than higher marks?

## FURTHER INVOLVEMENT

DIAMOND, STANLEY C., "Evaluation: The Dialogue of Learning," *Education* 94:3, Feb./Mar., 1974, pp. 237-241.

Suggests that the most desirable and effective form for informative evaluation is a narrative which spells out in detail what the student has achieved and what he has failed to achieve.

HENSON, KENNETH T., "Using Tests to Help Students," *Secondary Teaching: A Personal Approach*, F.E. Peacock Publishers, Inc., Itasca, IL., 1974, Chapter 6.

Summarizes the major concerns students have about testing and suggests two major functions of teacher made tests. The processes of test construction, administration, and evaluation are briefly discussed. A few case studies provide some real-life situations for analysis.

KIRSCHENBAUM, HOWARD, *Wad-Ja-Get?*, Hart Publishing Company, Inc., New York, 1971, 315 pp.

A tremendously interesting book which presents a novel approach to the study of grading systems. A few students question the grading system and the drama unfolds as the whole school and community become involved in the process of devising a better grading process. You have to resist turning to the back to see how the situation ends. Don't do it, though. It is worth reading from cover to cover and it is more exciting than a novel.

LACROIX, WILLIAM J., "Evaluating Learner Growth," *Man/Society/Technology* 33:5, February, 1974, pp. 133-6.

Teachers must evaluate, judge, and award grades but all too often they evaluate students merely to submit that time-honored course grade. The use of measurement instruments, their reliability and validity, and the role of instructional objectives are presented in the light of their use in educational evaluation.

LADAS, HAROLD, "Grades: Standardizing the Unstandardized Standard," *Phi Delta Kappan:* 56:3, Nov. 1974, pp. 185-187.

Defines the term "grade" and then submits its implications. Stresses that grades should help achieve student competence rather than sort out students. A good guideline for establishing a philosophy of grading.

MARSHALL, MAX S., "Pass or Question, but Describe," *Contemporary Education* 45:2, Winter, 1974, pp. 119-20. ERIC NO. EJ 097 022.

A sharp distinction is made between judgmental evaluation of a student and description of students' work and behavior. The author believes that a student's ranking will affect his relationship with the instructor and his performance.

SKAGER, RODNEY W., "Evaluation in the Classroom," in Allen, *The Teachers Handbook*, Scott, Foresman, and Co., Glenview, IL, 1971, pp. 259-268.

Submits that the teacher's conception of evaluation must shift radically in monitoring the effectiveness of instruction. Evaluation, then, becomes for the teacher a process of determining whether or not a given unit of instruction has been effective for a given student.

# SECTION III
# BECOMING INVOVED IN THE WIDER STUDENT WORLD

## Chapter Seven

## EDUCATION FOR STUDENTS
## WITH SPECIAL PROBLEMS

| | AGREE | DISAGREE | UNDECIDED |
|---|---|---|---|

### PRE-ASSESSMENT

### *How do you feel?*

1. A teacher can learn to recognize students who have special needs once he becomes familiar with some of the symptoms. — — —

2. Since most teachers have little or no preparation in special education, they should have no responsibility in helping these students. — — —

3. Every student, regardless of his ability, deserves the opportunity to be in school. — — —

4. Every teacher should demonstrate in his daily behavior the worth that he feels for all people. — — —

5. When a teacher has pity for a student, he should conceal this feeling. — — —

### *What do you think?*

1. When a teacher recognizes a student with a severe learning problem, he should refer him to a specialist. — — —

2. Both withdrawal and aggressiveness can be symptoms of a common need for attention and recognition. — — —

3. Students of low intellectual ability can be expected to have short attention spans. — — —

4. Every teacher needs to develop a routine or system for working with students who have special problems. — — —

5. The quality of the work of special students should never be compared to that of other pupils. — — —

131

## INTRODUCTION

As you look at the title of this chapter, you may be tempted to ask, "Why should I become concerned with students with special problems?" In today's schools all teachers are involved in some way with students who have particular needs. If you are anticipating teaching classes containing only average or above-average students, you may be disillusioned. The fact is that there are great variations among people, and even the so-called "normal" classes contain students who have unique problems.

This chapter is concerned with those students who vary from the average in a more pronounced way. Many of them will be in your classes full or part-time. There is an increasing interest in "mainstreaming" in special education today, whereby special students are encouraged to be in the same classes with the more typical student. The teacher may find that his class will include pupils with learning disabilities, cognition problems, and sometimes emotional problems. He must be able to identify the student who thinks slowly or has some other difficulty and learn to help him in class.

Once he has identified a student with special needs, the teacher should learn where to go for aid. The school system may have a school psychologist, psychometrist, or a counselor who can be of assistance. A quick referral can be the difference between adjustment and a continually deteriorating condition which may jeopardize the scholastic achievement and even the well being of a child.

The following experiences will reflect the demand for several types of decisions which teachers must make if they are to help those students who require the most assistance. Hopefully a look at these cases coupled with some direct contact with students with special needs will provide the insights necessary to help such individuals.

## IN THE CLASSROOM

### It's Too Embarrassing

New Mount High School recently added a program in speech therapy. Stephen Jacobs, a sophomore, was enrolled because of a stuttering problem. Stephen is an intelligent boy and usually makes good grades in school. He has recently become very unhappy and embarrassed about his stuttering and feels that his peers ridicule him. He has told Miss Foster, the speech therapist, that he doesn't think he needs any help because he "got along okay before."

Miss Foster recently received a call from Stephen's mother asking that he be dropped from further participation because he had expressed deep anxieties about therapy, and she believes that this may hinder him in his other school work. Miss Foster is well aware that Stephen is in need of assistance and that through professional aid he may learn to combat his stuttering problem. Her challenge is to convince the student and his parents that such a program will be helpful instead of harmful.

### Becoming Involved

1. What is a common misunderstanding of speech therapy shared by many parents and teachers?

2. Why do students who need speech therapy often prefer to do without it?

3. What can a classroom teacher do to help a person with a problem similar to this?

### Field Exploration

As a future teacher, your role may be to identify students who may have speech problems and refer them to a specialist. But, when a student refuses to adhere to your suggestion, what can be done?

Talk with a therapist about a teacher's responsibility to students with speech difficulties and ask her for suggested methods of psychologically "reaching" the student.

## Who Should Take Therapy?

Miss Little has been a speech therapist in the Ridgeway school system for six years. She has explained annually to the teachers and parents what procedure she uses to diagnose students' articulation and how they become enrolled in therapy groups. She also stresses that speech is comparable to any other course taken. The students will be graded on performance and are expected to drill every day.

As the school year began, Miss Little screened the students for their speech problems. Those who needed therapy were given a notification that they were to report to speech. The teachers were given a list of the time their students would be leaving.

On the first scheduled morning, Miss Little waited fifteen minutes for a group of students to arrive from Mr. Horn's class. When the students also failed to report for the next session, Miss Little became curious. Upon investigation, she learned that Mr. Horn would not permit the students to participate because he believed that therapy was unnecessary due to the fact that most students automatically correct their speech impediments. He also felt that those with serious handicaps would not be helped because there was neither adequate time nor special resources available to correct those difficulties.

Miss Little was quite concerned because she knew that she had to have a teacher's cooperation in order to conduct a successful program of therapy.

### Becoming Involved

1. What, if anything, has Miss Little done to provide communication between her office and the teachers?

2. What can a teacher in your area of specialty do to facilitate students with speech or hearing problems?

3. What is the responsibility of each teacher in this case?

### Field Exploration

Ask a speech therapist and an audiologist from your college or university to come to class and discuss how they would have teachers work cooperatively with them.

## Joe Is Back in School

Sandra Dix was not looking forward to the beginning of school today. "What am I going to do with Joe?" she thought. He had only recently returned to the classroom after a prolonged absence for treatment of an emotional disorder. He had received medication, but it seemed to have little benefit because he was as active as ever.

Sandra had to spend much of her time trying to control Joe instead of working with the other students in the class. He demanded attention and was in need of constant supervision. One morning he became incensed and threw a pair of scissors across the room. When Ms. Dix explained that such a move was dangerous, Joe became violent and tried to hit her. She forced him outside the classroom where he burst into tears.

Sandra first decided to try isolating Joe. This only resulted in emotional outbursts which could be heard in several nearby rooms. She then resolved to keep a complete case history hoping that such documentation would convince Mrs. Maloney, the principal, to refer the boy to a class for emotionally disturbed students. The principal reviewed the anecdotes and reluctantly agreed to accept Ms. Dix's recommendation that the student be transferred, although she knew that an appropriate type of school was not available in the system.

### Becoming Involved

1. What is the most valid justification for removing Joe from class?

2. How can a teacher be certain that a student like Joe has an emotional problem rather than merely a negative reaction to authority?

### Field Exploration

Invite a school psychologist or a university professor of adolescent or abnormal psychology to speak to the class on the symptoms of emotional instability. Then visit a class which is classified as emotionally handicapped and see how many symptoms you can recognize.


## Worry About Those Who Remain

Carolyn had problems with coordination which resulted in her being withdrawn and scared. Slow, deliberate progress was being made with her, though, as Mrs. Eisenberg and the school nurse worked to help her improve her self image.

The embarrassment of being different was quite difficult for her and she frequently missed school. One special teacher went to Carolyn's home to discuss her absences with her mother. She was rather unconcerned explaining that she had too many troubles of her own to worry about· Carolyn and school. She was unemployed and had very little money.

The next week, Carolyn walked into Mrs. Eisenberg's office to tell her good-bye. Tears came to her eyes as she said that her mother was planning to move to another state. Mrs. Eisenberg smiled and wished her a happy trip, but she had difficulty concealing her concern for this unfortunate child. Carolyn had made a few friends at the school and would now have to leave the people who were concerned about her. Even though Douglas High had failed to meet all of her needs, it had helped her to associate with people who cared for her welfare.

Mrs. Eisenberg discussed Carolyn's leaving with several other teachers during lunch. Some staff members suggested that she place her concern for the students that were remaining at Douglas and not with a student who was leaving. Mrs. Eisenberg was disturbed with their viewpoints, for it was difficult for her to forget this quiet little girl. This seemed like an empty rationalization because she knew that there would be more Carolyns and she feared that the faculty attitude was rather callous. Was it possible that she might be able to change a few opinions through her own example or should she avoid getting so involved with her students?

## Becoming Involved

1. What was the reason given by Mrs. Eisenberg's colleagues for their lack of concern toward Carolyn?

2. Do you believe that adolescents who are reserved and withdrawn are ignored?

3. What can you do to prevent apathy on behalf of fellow faculty members toward a withdrawn student who needs attention and help?

## Field Exploration

Arrange for a representative from the class to contact a principal. Ask him to provide you with the cumulative records of a former student who had some type of disability. Of course the name must be removed.

As a group, study the school history of this individual and discuss the teachers' comments about him. Discuss what you could do to help this person.

## The Two Susie's

Susie is a fifteen-year-old freshman who is bright but displays characteristics associated with emotional instability. On a given day, she could become completely stubborn and angry at the slightest provocation. She vented her anger at the new student teacher when she told her to get dressed for physical education class. When she was admonished, Susie remained undaunted and actually seemed to enjoy the extra attention which she was receiving.

For some unexplained reason, Susie's hostility subsequently abated and she became a very cooperative, sensitive girl. She was amiable and she began participating actively in class. Teaching was certainly much simpler with Susie in her more cooperative moods.

The peaceful state did not endure. One day as she was walking through the locker room before class, Miss Baker was aware that there was confusion in the area. When she heard some raucous behavior, she decided to move in. The appearance of the

137

teacher surprised the girls. Susie was obviously the ringleader and she was admonished for her actions. This provocation prompted Susie to become enraged at the teacher.

### Becoming Involved

1. Is it unusual for students to be both emotionally unstable and bright mentally?

2. Do you believe Susie really needed more attention?

3. Should teachers excuse behavior which is ordinarily unacceptable?

### Field Exploration

Ask a teacher or student teacher to identify a student who seems to have sudden unexplained changes of behavior. Observe that student for as long as possible. Can you identify any detectable reasons for the student's actions?

## WHAT THE EXPERTS SAY

Most preservice education programs in our universities do not require special education courses for regular classroom teachers; yet all classroom teachers have responsibilities for helping students with special learning difficulties. According to one author, the first and foremost of the teacher's responsibilities to these students is that of identifying them and then referring them to the experts.[1]

But, isn't it time for all teachers to learn to help the special education student move into the educational mainstream? How can this be achieved? In a 1973 publication, James R. Yates, Associate Director of the University Council for Educational Administration, Columbus, Ohio, reported a study which used a laboratory approach to prepare 30 teachers to work with special students. After 100 hours of instruction, the workshop was successful in in-

[1]K. T. Henson, *Secondary Teaching: A Personal Approach*, F. E. Peacock Publishers, Itasca, Il., 1974.

creasing the classroom teachers' knowledge about working with handicapped people and in convincing them that these students can be successfully integrated into regular classroom environments.[2]

Which special education students should be kept in regular classes? Several studies report that the current trend in dealing with special students is to have the regular classroom teacher deal with the individual's learning problems within the normal classroom situation.[3] But, of course, many students have handicaps which are so severe that it would be unwise to keep all such students in regular classrooms. How then can the teacher recognize those special students who should be dealt with in the regular classroom? Lilly (1970) defined the population who should be served by regular classroom teachers:

. . . the child whose problem can be seen as relatively mild, those children traditionally labeled as educable mentally retarded, emotionally disturbed, behaviorally disordered, educationally handicapped, learning disabled, or brain injured.

. . . referred from regular education programs because of some sort of teacher-perceived behavioral or learning problem . . . does not refer to children who have been called trainable mentally retarded, severely emotionally disturbed, multiply handicapped, or to children who are so obviously deviant that they have never been enrolled in any kind of normal program . . .

Cartwright[4] offers the following model for the regular classroom teacher:

a. Identify characteristics of individual learners that indicate special training or management procedures are required.

b. Specify relevant educational objectives for individual learners.

c. Select techniques for effective classroom management.

d. Choose and use specialized teaching strategies for reaching specific objectives for learners with varying behavioral learning characteristics.

[2]J. R. Yates, "Model For Preparing Classroom Teachers For Mainstreaming," *Exceptional Children* 39:471, March, 1973.

[3]C. A. Cartright, "Special Education In The Middle School," *Contemporary Education* 44: 218-21, Fall, 1973.

[4]Ibid

e. Choose and use special materials in association with specific strategies.

f.　Identify and use appropriate evaluation procedures.

g. Draw upon existing sources of information regarding specialized strategies and materials, and

h. Consult with available resource persons for assistance.

**In summary,** it may be observed that the experts see a more direct involvement of all teachers with students who have special problems. The teacher's task, although complicated, is to identify these students and help them to adjust to the school environment.

## DISCUSSION OF QUESTIONS

### It's Too Embarrassing

1. *What is a common misunderstanding of speech therapy shared by many parents and teachers?* That speech problems reflect such exceptionality that the student is peculiar.

2. *Why do students who need speech therapy often prefer to do without it?* Since parents often fail to understand speech defects and may be ashamed of or embarrassed about their children's problems, it is not surprising that many students share this feeling. Their reluctance to recognize, discuss, and admit their impediments prevents them from asking for help and from receiving it when it is offered.

3. *What can a classroom teacher do to help a person with a problem similar to this?* First, recognize that he is normal in most ways and treat him accordingly. Also, show empathy, but not sympathy in your contacts. Finally, make certain that his peers know that you accept him completely.

### Who Should Take Therapy?

1. *What, if anything, has Miss Little done to provide communication between her office and the teachers?* She has

developed a program for explaining the purpose of speech therapy to teachers and parents each year.

2. *What can a teacher in your area of specialty do to facilitate students with speech or hearing problems?* By involving each student daily in every lesson you can identify students with speech and hearing problems. The classroom teacher's main responsibility is that of referring students who need help. Also, you can be alert to and discourage comments from and among students who ridicule such personal traits.

3. *What is the responsibility of each teacher in this case?* Miss Little must see that Mr. Horn understands the purposes of therapy. She should also be aware of the scheduling problems which can occur. Mr. Horn must be responsible for cooperating with authorized programs.

### Joe Is Back in School

1. *What is the most valid justification for removing Joe from class?* He is interfering with the learning of others because he demands so much of the teacher's attention.

2. *How can a teacher be certain that a student like Joe has an emotional problem rather than merely a negative reaction to authority?* There should be records available which would indicate the severeness of his problem. The fact that he was out of school for an extended time would be a good clue in itself. If records are not available, the teacher should closely observe to see what prompts a student to have emotional outbursts. In some situations, other teachers can also provide some information based upon their experiences.

### Worry About Those Who Remain

1. *What was the reason given by Mrs. Eisenberg's colleagues for their lack of concern toward Carolyn?* They seemed to be saying that she should give attention to the others needing help instead of having concern for a girl who was leaving. In|fact,|this may

have been an excuse on their part because they did not really feel competent to help.

2. *Do you believe that adolescents who are reserved and withdrawn are ignored?* Unfortunately it is more typical than a person might assume, because many teachers do not realize that troubled people often are quiet and submissive. Also the cliche "The squeaky wheel gets the grease" can apply to schools. With so many difficult students to deal with, teachers do not seem to have time to provide for the student who does not cause problems.

3. *What can you do to prevent apathy on behalf of fellow faculty members toward a withdrawn student who needs attention and help?* One approach would be to point out any unique attributes of the student and to inform other teachers when the student makes progress in your room.

### The Two Susie's

1. *Is it unusual for students to be both emotionally unstable and bright mentally?* There is neither negative nor positive correlation between one's emotional stability and I.Q.

2. *Do you believe Susie really needed more attention?* Yes. However, care should be taken to see that it provides positive rather than negative reinforcement.

3. *Should teachers excuse behavior which is ordinarily unacceptable?* No. The student who has emotional problems must learn to live in society and society makes few exceptions for those who break its rules. By the same token, the teacher must also be aware of the fact that standard classroom techniques may not be as effective with students who have emotional problems.

## POST-ASSESSMENT

| | A G R E E | D I S A G R E E | U N D E C I D E D |
|---|---|---|---|

### How do you feel?

1. A teacher can learn to recognize students who have special needs once he becomes familiar with some of the symptoms. — — —

2. Since most teachers have little or no preparation in special education, they should have no responsibility in helping these students. — — —

3. Every student, regardless of his ability, deserves the opportunity to be in school. — — —

4. Every teacher should demonstrate in his daily behavior the worth that he feels for all people. — — —

5. When a teacher has pity for a student, he should conceal this feeling. — — —

### What do you think?

1. When a teacher recognizes a student with a severe learning problem, he should refer him to a specialist. — — —

2. Both withdrawal and aggressiveness can be symptoms of a common need for attention and recognition. — — —

3. Students of low intellectual ability can be expected to have short attention spans. — — —

4. Every teacher needs to develop a routine or system for working with students who have special problems. — — —

5. The quality of the work of special students should never be compared to that of other pupils. — — —

## SELF-ASSESSMENT

Now that you have completed the pre- and post-assessment, compare them. Check the items where there is disagreement between responses. Examine your reasons for any changes. What influenced that change?

1. How are special students different from the so-called "normal" students?

2. What are your own strengths and limitations in identifying and helping students with special problems?

3. What is the teacher's obligation to special students?

## FURTHER INVOLVEMENT

DAILEY, REBECCA F., "Dimensions and Issues in '74; Tapping into the Special Education Grapevine," *Exceptional Children* 40;503-6, April, 1974.

The author summarizes the results of a telephone interview survey of over 80 leaders in the field of special education. She attempted to identify the most important problems and issues in the field along with current activities and projects which are considered significant by the leaders. The main issue, that of assimilating students into the mainstream, concerns all who are involved with education.

ASSOCIATION FOR SUPERVISION AND CURRICULUM DEVELOPMENT, "Learning Disability; Role of the School" *Educational Leadership* Vol. 32, No. 8.

This complete issue is devoted to explaining the role of the school in providing for children with learning disabilities. It begins by defining disabilities, and proceeds to explore various ways in which teachers and other school personnel can work together to meet these needs.

FINDLEY, WARREN G., and BRYAN, MIRIAM M., *The Pros and Cons of Ability Grouping*, Phi Delta Kappa, Bloomington, IN., 1975.

Is ability grouping a more efficient way of teaching? Or is it subtle segregation? The authors explore four alternatives to ability grouping.

QUAY, H. C., "Special Education; Assumptions, Techniques, and Evaluative Criteria," *Exceptional Child* 40:165-70, November, 1973.

This overview examines the nature of educational exceptionality as well as remedial techniques and instructional methods in special education.

ROGOW, S., and DAVID, C., "Special Education; Symposium," *Phi Delta Kappan* 55:514-60, April, 1974.

A special issue on special education. Articles on trends and issues, innovative programs, and the future of special education. This symposium presents a thorough look at the situation.

# Chapter Eight

## THE CHALLENGE OF THE DRUG CULTURE

### PRE-ASSESSMENT
*How do you feel?*

|  | AGREE | DISAGREE | UNDECIDED |
|---|---|---|---|
| 1. Drugs in secondary schools present a serious problem for teachers. | — | — | — |
| 2. Teachers should give marked attention in their instruction to the drug problem. | — | — | — |
| 3. The ends justify the means in regard to the elimination of the drug culture even if it means that a teacher should exaggerate about the effects of drugs. | — | — | — |
| 4. Because drugs present so many possible dangers, teachers must closely monitor their classes for drug-related irregularities. | — | — | — |
| 5. The teacher who moralizes about drugs is ineffective in convincing students of their danger. | — | — | — |

### What do you think?

|  | AGREE | DISAGREE | UNDECIDED |
|---|---|---|---|
| 1. Drugs are substances which, when improperly used, have the potential of permanently damaging the body physically, mentally, and emotionally. | — | — | — |
| 2. The drug problem is a "middle-class" phenomenon and is not a serious concern among lower or upper class students. | — | — | — |
| 3. The motivation for students' taking drugs is very similar to their reasons for smoking, drinking, and becoming involved in gangs. | — | — | — |
| 4. Adults tend to overreact with students in regard to drugs because they assume that consumption is habit forming and may ruin the lives of the young. | — | — | — |
| 5. If students understand the nature of drugs, they will more volitionally terminate their use. | — | — | — |

145

## INTRODUCTION

The concern over the danger of drug use has prompted an extensive reaction in our society. The use of drugs by young people is regarded as a serious problem in all areas of the nation. . .A total of 59 percent of the parents who have children now attending public schools say that the use of drugs by young people locally is a serious problem.[1]

Every major group in the population, according to Gallup, would require students to attend a program on the effects of drugs and alcohol.[2] The result of this attitude has caused drug abuse information to flourish with a concentrated emphasis being placed on drug education today.

The schools have responded by incorporating drug instruction in their curricula. New courses of study have been developed and sophisticated teaching resources have appeared in an effort to convince students that drugs are harmful. Inservice education programs have been designed to acquaint all teachers with the nature of the problem and to suggest ways that they can be aware of drug use in their own classes.

Some teachers and pupils feel that drug information in the schools has reached the overkill level. The repetition of admonitions and scare techniques has sometimes resulted in the students becoming disgusted, blase, or just plain oblivious of the warnings. "Why is everyone so excited?" they **ask.** "Adults drink and alcohol is a drug, but no one seems very alarmed about curbing that practice. And what are they doing to control the smoke that flows out the door of the teachers' lounge? Don't they know that cigarettes are both habit forming and harmful to health? Why is this double standard being applied?"

As the arguments continue, the classroom teacher has to cope with the existing situation. What is the appropriate reaction when a student admits to being on drugs? What is the best course of action for a teacher who suspects that a pupil is "stoned"? Should he

---

[1]George Gallup, "Seventh Annual Gallup Poll of Public Attitudes Toward Education," *Phi Delta Kappan* 57:5, pp. 227-241, December, 1975.

[2] Ibid.

relate his own instruction to this problem or dismiss it as the responsibility of health education or parental guidance? The following case studies describe situations which are related to the problems of drug usage and their manifestation in school. What implications are there for the teaching situation?


## IN THE CLASSROOM

### Wound Up and Strung Out

Normal High School has a good college preparation program but is also interested in non-college bound students. There are a variety of programs for the non-academic student, but the most popular one seems to be the vocational machine class, taught by Mr. Merrick, who is highly regarded.

The class meets for three hours every afternoon. Since it was first offered four years ago, more students have applied for it than can be accommodated. Mr. McDonald, the principal, suggested that Mr. Merrick accept only the students who are sincerely interested in the field. As a result, it has been a rather selective group.

Greg Cantrell was an eager student initially, but he soon changed. He became an erratic worker, who would perform well on occasion but would not get involved at all at other times. Since his class is operated like an actual industrial shop, Mr. Merrick dealt with the problem as he thought that an employer would. He explained to Greg that he would have to display greater interest or he would be dropped from the class. Greg's working habits improved so much that it appeared he had overcome his changeable approach. He was almost a model student except that he would easily become agitated if something did not function properly. Once when he became angry with one of the machines, he began kicking and cursing it. Mr. Merrick told him to go into the classroom and regain his self control.

Since Greg had seemed excitable all day, Mr. Merrick resolved to watch him closely. After two hours he decided to take a short break and sit in the classroom, where he could look through a large window into the laboratory and peruse the entire area. He had just begun looking over some test papers when he caught a glimpse of Greg striking the lathe with a large hammer. He ran to him and grabbed the hammer and as he did, he saw that Greg had lost some muscle coordination. Was he strung out?

### Becoming Involved

1. What behaviors indicated that Greg might be under the influence of drugs?

2. Is this sufficient to prove that he actually is on drugs?

3. Should Greg be suspended so that a more serious student could enroll in this popular class?

### Field Exploration

Ask a local social worker or a local law enforcement official to visit your class and discuss the drug issue. Perhaps he can indicate the extent to which drugs are affecting adolescents in your community. He may even be able to arrange for you to talk with adolescents who are consuming drugs. From this information make a list of behaviors which a teacher might observe which are symptomatic of drug consumption.

## Preacher's Kid

Todd was a fourteen-year-old minister's son who appeared to be a normal junior high school student. He was popular with his classmates and seemed to get along well with teachers. His class rank was well above the school median.

Since Todd apparently adjusted easily to school, it was quite a surprise when his disposition suddenly changed. He would often stare into space and speak in a despondent tone of voice. His grades began to decline for no apparent reason, and he became alienated from his friends. His teachers reported that he had lost interest and was not getting his work done. The guidance director thought that he was undergoing one of those stages of growing up.

Finally, a student teacher who was concerned about Todd suggested that they talk. Todd accepted his proposition with the assurance that the conversation would be confidential. Carefully and cautiously he explained his problem: He had become bored with life and about a month ago he started searching for something new. He did not know what he wanted, but he was looking for excitement. He concluded by saying that he had decided to use drugs. He indicated that he started out with the light stuff and now was on harder drugs.

The student teacher was not prepared for this admission. How could a decent fourteen-year-old boy who had so much going for him turn to drugs? There were other questions which had to be answered: Was he to get outside help in trying to solve Todd's problem? If so, would this require divulging the conversation which he had promised to keep confidential? Should Todd's parents be notified? Exactly what should or could a student teacher do?

### Becoming Involved

1. Should the student teacher disclose Todd's situation?
2. If you were Todd's teacher and you knew of his problem, how would you approach it?
3. Should the student teacher counsel with Todd?

### Field Exploration

Do schools have any standard procedure which is used for counseling students who are involved with drugs? Try to see if such practices exist by talking with the counselors at the school.

## Don't Let Them Follow You Home

Miss Brentwood was an intern in a large educational complex which subscribes to the philosophy of individualized instruction. Although her subject did not adapt as easily to this style as some other areas, she attempted to be informal and open with her students. They responded positively and seemed to be interested in school. Much of her free time was consumed by people from her class who wanted to talk with her. Topics ranged from discussions about school work to some rather personal concerns.

After a while, some students began to show up at Miss Brentwood's apartment after hours. She was concerned at first, but she felt that friendliness toward adolescents was not to necessarily conform to the hours of the school day. Student visits became more frequent and sometimes the sessions turned into lively discussions related to the classroom topics. They appeared mature and pleasant, and Miss Brentwood came to feel that her extracurricular interaction with her pupils was definitely beneficial.

The experience continued to go well for this enthusiastic young intern until one Friday evening when three students dropped by just as Miss Brentwood was preparing to leave. When she learned that they did not have a ride home until nine o'clock, she indicated that it would be all right for them to stay at her apartment until then. She had no reservations because she felt that they could handle responsibility.

When she arrived home that evening, she found a note on her door directing that she see the apartment manager as soon as possible. He informed her that earlier in the evening he had noticed an odor coming from her door when he was walking past. Upon entering to check out the scent, he discovered two young girls and a boy smoking marijuana in the living room. He had called their parents who had come immediately to pick them up. He said that his observation of the parents' behavior led him to the conclusion that they would report the whole incident to the school officials the following Monday.

### Becoming Involved

1. What mistake(s) did Miss Brentwood make?

2. In what way(s) was Miss Brentwood innocent?

3. What observations can be made about the drug scene from this case?

### Field Exploration

It is now Monday morning. The apartment manager was correct. The principal has just sent word for Miss Brentwood to come to the office to discuss this matter with the parents of the students, the dean, and himself. Assign parts for each person participating in this meeting. Directly following this meeting, the remaining students will decide the fate of Miss Brentwood.

## A Star Falls

Reggie Reynolds was a popular student and the star of the basketball team. He was a friend to his co-players and classmates and he was well liked by the school staff. He was "Mr. Clean" as far as his acquaintances were concerned, and he was an example for many younger students in the school.

The week before the annual tournament began, Reggie was approached by Jerry Gillespie, a reserve on the team who said that he needed to secure some grass for a friend. Did Reggie know of any source? Reggie said that he knew of a few boys in the school who smoked pot and that he observed that some transactions had taken place. He was quick to point out that he did not want to become involved.

Jerry said that he had no way of making connections without suspicion because he rode the bus and could not come back into town to make contacts after school. He asked Reggie if he would get it for him so that he could deliver it to a friend. Although it was against his better judgment, Reggie felt that it might be better to cooperate rather than create any possible friction among players near tournament time.

"Okay," Reggie said, "I will talk with Bill and it will be in my car after school tomorrow." Jerry resisted, "I think it would avoid suspicion if you brought it to my locker rather than risk being seen in the parking lot in daylight." Reggie agreed and they arranged to meet at the locker at 2:45 on the following day.

As Reggie walked toward the locker area at the appointed time, he was unexpectedly met by the athletic director. Reggie spoke as they passed in the hall; then the athletic director called to him and asked what was in his coat pocket. He was completely stunned. Assuming that honesty was the best policy, he admitted that he had some grass for a friend.

Now it was the teacher's turn to be aghast, because he had merely asked the question in jest. However he felt that he had no alternative but to report the incident. The principal summoned Reggie and asked him to identify the student who had asked for the marijuana.

Jerry was identified and brought to the office also. When he was confronted, he denied all the accusations and implied that Reggie felt that his position on the ball team was being threatened by Jerry's recent success in the last two games. Jerry continued his denials and was eventually sent back to class.

The principal then called Reggie's parents, the superintendent, the athletic director, and the coach into the office. When everyone arrived, the principal suggested that Reggie should be expelled from school for three days and suspended from all athletic activities indefinitely.

### Becoming Involved

1. Was Reggie's guilt as serious as it would have been had he been using drugs himself?

2. What seemed to cause Reggie to become involved in an activity which he was basically opposed to?

### Field Exploration

How much do teachers know about how drugs are exchanged and who uses drugs? As a group in class, prepare a few questions which will help to determine what teachers know. Talk with a few teachers and compare answers.

### You Can't Beat Experience

Kevin was enthusiastic, idealistic and energetic. He liked teaching the health class and had enjoyed the give-and-take dialogue with the students. He had gained their respect with his thorough knowledge of the subject. His anecdotes about some experiences provided a lively environment for the study of a subject that is generally considered a "drag" by the students.

Kevin came to his fourth week in the classroom and announced that they would begin with a study of drugs the following week. He endured the scattered groans throughout the class and indicated that he had experienced several situations involving drugs and that he knew a few things about the matter which were not covered in the book. "I think that you may be interested in this."

The group was challenged by his comments, although they were not convinced that any adult could really understand the drug culture. So, in order to test the teacher, several of the students became stoned during the preceding lunch break, walked into the room, sat down, and displayed some behaviors which are indicative of drug usage.

Kevin knew the drug scene, and he detected the odor of grass immediately. He studied his class and realized that as many as ten or twelve people were under the influence of drugs. The bell rang and it was time for him to begin his new unit of study on narcotics.

### Becoming Involved

1. Should Kevin risk destroying the good rapport that he had with this class by exposing the ten?

2. What can the teacher do to make the drug unit more exciting?

### Field Exploration

Talk with the curriculum director of a school. What formal instructional activities are provided about drugs in the system? Where do they start? What evidence have they accumulated to indicate that the instruction is of any value? Do the answers support the conclusions that there may be too much instruction in this area?

## WHAT THE EXPERTS SAY

Today's teacher will most likely be confronted with the drug problem in some form. The easiest course of action is to evade the whole complex question and let the "experts" handle it, but the teacher should not ignore it because the student is his prime responsibility. The boy or girl in the classroom may look to the teacher for advice, help, or even friendship.[3] The more knowledgeable that he becomes about this subject, the better equipped he will be to give understanding when it is required.

What are the generalities in regard to the practice of using drugs? The consensus seems to be that drug use often begins in the lower grade levels and peaks during the upper high school years.[4] It has been reported that 59 percent of addicts at the Lexington Hospital started using drugs before age twenty-one.[5] Some experts speculate that more than half of the population in a secondary school have at least experimented with drugs in some form. Two studies[6,7] have described drug use as a social problem, relating to such conditions as poor housing and limited educational and recreational facilities.

Is drug abuse concentrated in any particular type of community? Braxton and Yonker[8] reported that during the spring, summer, and fall of 1971, 569 students of grades five to eleven in five cities, from very small to very large were surveyed to identify the effects of urbanization, grade level, ethnic background, poverty, and sex upon the adolescent's knowledge of and participation with drugs. The study found that students of cities exceeding one-half million people knew less about drugs than students of cities of 50,000 to one-half million and small cities of five to fifty thousand in population. Predominately white groups scored higher than did their black countergroups. Students in groups whose

[3]Milton Strumpf, "Can One Teacher Help?" *Drug Education* 3:3, Fall, 1973, p. 297.

[4]Nicholas Galli, "Patterns of Student Drug Use," *Journal of Drug Education* 4:2, Summer, 1974, p. 237.

[5]William J. Webster, "Trends In Reported Drug Usage Among Public School Children," *The Journal of Experimental Education* 42:2, Winter, 1973., pp. 80-86.

[6]Dana L. Farnsworth, "Drug Use for Pleasure: A Complex Social Problem," *The Journal of School Health*, March, 1973, pp. 153-158.

[7]Jack Soroda and Laurence Schulman, "Coping With Newark's Drug Abuse Dilemma," *The Journal of School Health*, Feb., 1973, pp. 127-8.

[8]E. R. Braxton, and R. J. Yonker, "Does Being Urban, Poor, Black, or Female Affect Youth's Knowledge and/or Attitudes Relating to Drugs?" *Journal of School Health* 43: 185-8, March, 1973.

family averaged over $4,000 a year scored higher than students in groups whose family averaged less. There was no significant difference in scores between male and female participants.

In addition to the demographic information, the study found that:

1. All students were concerned about the sale and distribution of drugs, and a high percentage favored stiff jail sentences for persons engaged in illegal sales.

2. All students were actively interested in helping a friend who was having drug problems.

3. Most students would seek help for a friend or self, first from doctors and ministers and second from teachers and parents.

4. Many students would report information to the police regarding illegal sales.

A review of the cases in this chapter may cause the reader to wonder why students use drugs. Hollister[9] lists the following reasons why adolescents use drugs:

1. rebellion toward parents.

2. personal feelings of inadequacy.

3. for pleasurable thrills.

4. to reduce boredom.

5. as a solace for fears and doubts.

6. as escape from responsibility.

How successful have schools been in alleviating drug use through instructional programs? The results seem to indicate more bad news than good news. Experts are saying that most drug programs are so bad that schools would be well advised to junk them.[10] For example, the National Education Association Task Report on Drug Education concluded that "the majority of programs are superficial and educationally poor. Some of the programs, because of false statements made by misinformed or uninformed educators, could very well have contributed to the increase of drug use in this society."

Other criticisims allege that drug abuse films in the schools

[9]G. Hollister, "Why Adolescents Drink and Use Drugs," *PTA Magazine* 63:2-5, 1969.

[10]Bernard Bard, "The Failure of our School Drug Abuse Programs," *Phi Delta Kappan* 57:4, December, 1975, pp. 251-255.

are full of errors and that drug education has reached a state of overkill in today's schools. It is crisis oriented, tends toward exaggeration and inaccuracy, relies heavily on sermons and warning that drugs are dangerous and illegal, and often tells youngsters what they already know. Indeed, classroom instruction probably broadens students' knowledge about drugs.

If this is correct, what should the schools do? Instead of pouring money into drug education, the schools ought to invest money in methods of increasing teacher accountability, providing more innovative curricula, and strengthening students' achievement levels. Drug use is often an adolescent's response to a pattern of "systematic failure ranging from boring, dreadfully conducted school experiences to punitive family experiences to general social chaos and dislocation."

Instead of using scare techniques, experts suggest programs which are designed to raise student achievement levels, which select teachers who are really knowledgeable about the narcotics scene and thus respected by students, and possibly "peer-group" programs which are based on the assumptions that students know more about drugs than do most teachers and that fellow students will trust them more than adults. In other words, we need more people who know about drugs and who are dedicated to helping students improve their self concept in ways other than escape to drugs.

A teacher can be a part in alleviating drug abuse, but he may inadvertently also be part of the cause through poor teaching practices, failure to really know his students, or failure to know about drugs. He should be able to make sharp distinctions between drugs, because the user is capable of doing so. Only then can he be really knowledgeable about the problems encountered by the users.[11] This is a complicated task which cannot be explored in a cursory fashion.

[11]Michael R. McKee, "Main Street, U.S.A.: Fact and Fiction About Drugs Abuse," *Journal of Drug Education* 3:3, Fall, 1973, p. 275.

## DISCUSSION OF QUESTIONS

### Wound Up and Strung Out

1. *What behaviors indicated that Greg might be under the influence of drugs?* His behavior was erratic and there were times when he seemed unable to control himself. The teacher observed that his hands were trembling at times and he seemed to lack coordination.

2. *Is this sufficient to prove that he actually is on drugs?* No. It is sufficient to suspect that drugs might be the cause. It is also reason to cause the teacher to investigate the boy's profile in a more complete way in order to determine the cause of his actions.

3. *Should Greg be suspended so that a more serious student could enroll in this popular class?* Not necessarily. Greg periodically was showing signs of improved attention. Suspension might tend to perpetuate the problem. Since the teacher admonition led to temporary improvement, it may be assumed that further teacher action would continue to be helpful.

### Preacher's Kid

1. *Should the student teacher disclose Todd's situation?* No. Exposing him would result in his losing the confidence that he now holds in the student teacher. Although Todd needs professional help, he probably would not benefit if it were forced upon him. The student teacher should try to persuade Todd to seek the help of a professional. In the meanwhile the student teacher can ask for the advice of an expert without revealing the student's name.

2. *If you were Todd's teacher and you knew of his problem, how would you approach it?* Hopefully you have considered your own unique strengths and have thought of a way to apply them to Todd's problem. Generally, it appears that the perceptive teacher would attempt to get the student more involved with and excited about learning.

3. *Should the student teacher counsel with Todd?* The stu-

dent teacher should realize his limitations. He possibly should spend his energy and talent encouraging Todd to see a specialist on his own initiative. However, he may best be able to achieve that goal by serving as Todd's confidant.

### Don't Let Them Follow You Home

1. *What mistake(s) did Miss Brentwood make?* For her protection and theirs she should not have permitted the students to visit her at her apartment.

2. *In what ways was Miss Brentwood innocent?* She was not aware of their intentions to use drugs in her apartment. She had not encouraged or sanctioned their use of drugs.

3. *What observations can be made about the drug scene from this case?* Students may exploit the close friendship with a teacher; pupils may be presumed to be guilty of smoking marijuana on the basis of the suspicions of a non-professional; and parents may tend to blame teachers for not exercising adequate supervision.

### A Star Falls

1. *Was Reggie's guilt as serious as it would have been had he been using drugs himself?* In a strict legal sense, it probably is. When one considers the entire context, however, it is obvious that his being naive is not as serious as actual drug consumption.

2. *What seemed to cause Reggie to become involved in an activity which he was basically opposed to?* He seemed to be primarily concerned with preserving harmonious peer relationships for the benefit of the athletic squad. This seemed to have more priority than his reservations about being involved in exchanging drugs.

### You Can't Beat Experience

1. *Should Kevin risk destroying the good rapport that he had with this class by exposing the ten?* Kevin must give priority to

obeying the laws of the school and society. Also, he has an obligation to the remainder of the class who might be rather bored or irritated at those ten. He certainly will have to make the students aware of the fact that he knows what is occurring.

2. *What can the teacher do to make the drug unit more exciting?* Although students are weary of hearing lectures on drugs, they may not be tired of talking about drugs. The teacher could begin the study unit by taking whatever time necessary to let the students express their knowledge and their attitudes toward drugs. As a group they could begin compiling a list of objective evidence of positive and negative effects of each type of drug.

## POST-ASSESSMENT

A G R E E    D I S A G R E E    U N D E C I D E D

### *How do you feel?*

1. Drugs in secondary schools present a serious problem for teachers. — — —

2. Teachers should give marked attention in their instruction to the drug problem. — — —

3. The ends justify the means in regard to the elimination of the drug culture, even if it means that a teacher should exaggerate about the effects of drugs. — — —

4. Because drugs present so many possible dangers, teachers must closely monitor their classes for drug-related irregularities. — — —

5. The teacher who moralizes about drugs is ineffective in convincing students of their danger. — — —

### *What do you think?*

1. Drugs are substances which, when improperly used, have the potential of permanently damaging the body—physically, mentally, and emotionally. — — —

2. The drug problem is a "middle-class" phenomenon and is not a serious concern among lower or upper class students. — — —

3. The motivation for students' taking drugs is very similar to their reasons for smoking, drinking, and becoming involved in gangs. — — —

4. Adults tend to overreact with students in regard to drugs because they assume that consumption is habit forming and may ruin the lives of the young. — — —

5. If students understand the nature of drugs, they will more volitionally terminate their use. — — —

## SELF-ASSESSMENT

Now that you have completed the post-assessment, compare your pre- and post-assessment scores. Check those items where there is disagreement between responses. Examine your reasons for any changes. What influenced each change?

1. What is the role of the teacher in regard to:
    a. teaching about drugs?
    b. counseling students concerning drugs?
2. What do you believe about:
    a. the extent to which drugs are consumed in schools?
    b. the attitudes of students toward drugs?
    c. the potential danger of various drugs?

## FURTHER INVOLVEMENT

ANONYMOUS, "Drugs--Problem or Solution?" *Independent School Bulletin*, 33:29-31, May 1974.

The author asked to remain anonymous in order to protect the confidentiality of his study of a group of young people in an upper middle-class community. His results submit that drugs are an attempted solution to a problem rather than the problem itself. The author offers ideas for fighting the problem of drug users. A good guideline for teachers.

FEJER, DIANNE, and SMART, REGINALD G., "The Knowledge About Drugs, Attitudes Towards Them and Drug Use Rates of High School Students," *Journal of Drug Education* 3:4, Winter, 1973, pp. 377-387. ERIC NO. EJ 090 919.

A survey of attitudes and knowledge toward drugs involving 4,693 high school students. Questions were raised concerning the value of providing factual information as a method of deterring drug use.

HARNETT, ARTHUR L., "How We Do It," *Journal of School Health* 43:10, December, 1973, pp. 658-662.

A description of how one school approaches the problem of drug information in a way designed to keep students interested. Good reading for any teacher candidate.

LANE, DAVID A., "Individuals and Systems; Aspects of Educational Issues in Drug Dependence," *Educational Research*, 16:52-7, November 1973.

Mr. Lane looks at the way drug education helps individuals with their problems and finds that the school can be an important influence both positively and negatively. He suggests both group and individual approaches to drug education.

NICKERSON, CARL J., "An Examination of Five Difficult Issues Related to School Drug Problems," *Journal of School Health*, 42:441-445, October 1972.

The author examines five drug issues which seem to receive little attention at professional meetings: (1) self-fulfilling prophecy, (2) drug traffic on campus, (3) emergency care, (4) drug-experienced resource people, (5) profiteering. This is a guide to some practical problems coupled with a few suggestions on how to cope.

THORNBURY, HERSHEL, "Adolescent and Drugs: An Overview" *Journal of School Health* 43:640-4, December 1973.

The author looks at several forms of drug usage with special emphasis on alcohol, nonaddictive drugs, and the hallucinogens. One interesting aspect of the article is that he provides explanation of why individuals opt for certain types of drugs. The concluding three suggestions concerning making drug education relevant to youth may be worthwhile.

# Chapter Nine

## THE TEACHER AND MINORITIES

**PRE-ASSESSMENT**

*How do you feel?*

1. Middle-class values are the standards by which school performance should be evaluated. — — —

2. The conflict of black and white values presents unmanageable tasks for the teacher when the groups are integrated. — — —

3. Teachers who work with minority-group pupils need specialized professional training. — — —

4. Any teacher who works with minorities must be prepared to cope with an additional syndrome of problems. — — —

5. The school is the best, and perhaps the only institution which can provide the opportunity for divergent groups to get to know and understand each other. — — —

*What do you think?*

1. The problem of minorities in the school encompasses any group which feels alienated because any majority tends to suppress the rights of a minority. — — —

2. Most racial incidents in schools are prompted by seemingly innocuous acts. — — —

3. Problems with minorities in schools often result from the lack of a relevant curriculum. — — —

4. The rights of the majority should take precedence over the demands of the minority. — — —

5. The typical school stresses conformity to its standards and has little tolerance for groups with differing views or goals. — — —

## INTRODUCTION

Education for minorities has received considerable emphasis in teaching circles during the past few years. Spurred on by federal legislation and court decisions, educational programs have been designed to try to improve the status of underprivileged groups. The teacher now finds himself involved with programs ranging from compensatory education to new curricula which stress the contributions of minority groups to our society. He may also discover that a large number of pupils have been bused to the school in order to achieve racial balance.

When classrooms contain representatives from one or more groups, there will be people who have differing values above and beyond those in the normal adult-adolescent relationship. It is a challenge for both the teachers and pupils to learn to relate to and tolerate students from various racial and cultural groups. The teacher's role is not so much that of expecting all students to be like him; it is to help each individual discover his unique potential and develop it to the maximum.

The typical educator is white and middle class. How does this person react to pupils from a group which displays behaviors which seem strange or even hostile? The Department of Health, Education, and Welfare recently reported that hundreds of school districts are applying more severe disciplinary measures to minority students than to white children. Furthermore, minority children are receiving a disproportionate number of discipline actions in the form of expulsions and suspensions.

The fact that multicultural classes have built-in problems is as obvious as is the fact that multicultural classes possess unique opportunities for young people to learn how to become modern Americans.[1] The following case studies describe some of the phenomena which occur when members of different groups fail to understand each other. Will these experiences help you, a future teacher, to understand the opportunities as well as the problems and challenges of working with a broad cross section of people in the schools?

[1]Kenneth T. Henson, "American Schools vs. Cultural Pluralism," *Educational Leadership* 32:405-08, March, 1973.

## IN THE CLASSROOM
### The Phantom Strikes Twice

Lincoln School observed Black History Week as a part of the national emphasis on the cultural contribution of minorities. The art students had made posters of famous blacks and placed them on the walls and bulletin boards of the school.

During the second day of Black History Week some of the posters were defaced. Mustaches, glasses, and beards had been added. Teeth had been blackened out on some pictures and cigars had been drawn on others. No one knew who had done this. Some teachers went from poster to poster adjusting the faces and erasing those marks that could be removed.

The following day this mishap occurred again and once more the posters were repaired. Several of the faculty wondered how they could stop it from happening again, because they felt that this relatively harmless act might precipitate conflict among the students.

### Becoming Involved

1. What symbolic significance was there in the act of defacing pictures?

2. What evidence is there that some faculty members may be neglecting their responsibility in curbing this destruction?

3. As a teacher at Lincoln, what could you do to help lessen the problem?

### Field Exploration

Invite a group of six or eight students from local schools who represent cultures other than that which dominates this class membership. Questions to be asked of them should include: In what ways do you feel that others show little respect for your people? What behaviors most clearly indicate that members of other ethnic groups do respect you? What qualities and feelings do you possess which are often ignored by members of other cultures?

## Talk Only to Your Brother

Superior High School is a fairly large school which has a small black population. Mr. Engle, Superior's principal, was happy to have Martin Kerlin as a teacher, not only because of his teaching ability, but also because he was the only black person on his staff who could effectively double as a counselor. Since Martin relates easily to other people, he is frequently called on to help solve some of the black-white problems among students.

Martin first established communication with one of the less cooperative black students when he observed him making some rather direct advances to a girl in the hall. He calmly asked Fred to meet him for a conference during his lunch period. Fred disclosed some of his personal frustrations and admitted that he disliked being in the same school "with a lot of honks."

The following day the school presented a play during convocation. Fred and his friend, Jesse, showed contempt for the whole affair by laughing, shouting, and making derisive remarks during the program. When their teacher asked them to leave the auditorium, they made a big issue of being singled out because they are black. When Mr. Engle confronted them, they indicated that they would not talk to any white teacher and that they would only talk with the "brother" who teaches. Mr. Kerlin was summoned to the office for assistance.

As he entered, he asked the rest of the staff to leave. As the door closed, he turned, faced the boys, and looked at them for a long period of time before he uttered a word. Then he started talking to them in their vernacular, telling the surprised pair that they were acting the way the white students expected them to act and if they were going to continue with such gross behavior, they were going to cause all blacks in the school to be embarrassed. The students attempted a rejoinder, but their arguments did not persuade the one they regard as a "brother."

### Becoming Involved

1. What evidence is there to suggest that the problem is racial?

166

2. How does this incident suggest that schools with black students should have black teachers?

3. Was Mr. Kerlin's approach to this problem a wise one?

### Field Exploration

When you next visit a high school campus, ask the school counselor or dean of students to arrange for you to talk to some of the students who have a maximum of racial conflicts with teachers and other students. Through informal talks try to identify some common areas of concern. If the class is divided into groups, each section can interview representatives from a particular ethnic group. Tape your interview on a cassette recorder.

During the following class meeting(s) replay each tape to the class while they think of suggestions for working in specific ways with future students from each ethnic group.

### Recipe for a Dropout

Anyone can find himself identified with the minority, as Mark Kinney discovered when he enrolled in the school's advanced foods class. He did not initially object to being the only boy in the class because he enjoys cooking and hopes to operate his own restaurant some day. His counselor advised him to enroll in the class as background for the vocational food service program which he planned to take.

Advanced foods proved to be a large, overcrowded class containing twenty-six sophomores. Mrs. Alexander stated that she considered the presence of a boy in this class to be a nuisance. She criticized him in front of the class and ascribed low marks for his lab work. She pointed out that Mark is uncooperative in class and is careless.

Mark's enthusiasm for foods seemed to be deteriorating. Both his test and lab grades dropped to poor levels. His other teachers indicated that he had lost interest in their classes too. Mark had often taken a leadership role in his classes, but now he isolates himself from his former friends. He also started to miss classes frequently, especially on food lab days. Mrs. Alexander had given

167

Mark after-school conference slips twice, but he did not show up for either one. She referred him to a counselor.

Mark told the counselor that he hated to cook and that he did not want to remain in the foods class. As far as he was concerned, cooking was for girls. The counselor told him that he must remain in the class because it was a school policy that classes could not be dropped during the middle of the semester. Mark then accused Mrs. Alexander of being prejudiced. He says that other pupils will back him up. He also insists that he will drop out of school if he is coerced to stay in class.

### Becoming Involved

1. What evidence is there that Mrs. Alexander is prejudiced against boys?

2. What behavior does Mark practice which suggests that his interest in cooking is diminishing?

3. This case describes apparent discrimination against a boy. What other examples of sex discrimination are practiced in the schools?

### Field Exploration

Visit a home economics teacher. Ask her how many boys she has in each of her classes. Then ask her if she does anything special for the boys. Make the same inquiry of a teacher in a field that previously was populated by boys only and now enrolls a few girls. What conclusions can be drawn concerning the differing situations presented by members of the opposite sex?

During the following session, each person should be prepared to share his findings with the class and to indicate if he believes each is an accurate observation.

## Manuel's Second Charge

During his first two weeks of teaching, Mike was a bit annoyed at some of his seventh-grade students at Grande Middle School. Since he was accustomed to the silence of the college classroom, he was bothered by the squirming, the constant

168

sounds of pencils pounding on desk tops, shoes shuffling, and desks moving and squeaking back and forth. He also was unaccustomed to working with students who represent minority groups, and he felt uncomfortable with some of their mannerisms. He talked with Mrs. Langly about the problem and she had given him a few hints about how to stop the noise as well as to interpret some cultural conditions which affect youngsters whose background is Latin-American.

Mike proceeded to discuss the day's lesson with the students. He had to remind a few of the students that they were a little noisy and were distracting others. One of these students was Manuel, who was censured three times during the period. Manuel objected to being singled out, saying that the teacher was picking on him.

Ten minutes later, Manuel was caught trying to push the chair of the boy in front of him. Mike told him to remain after class, but Manuel objected and stated flatly that he was not going to be the only one to stay, because there were others who were goofing around too. He challenged Mike with, "You don't like the color of my skin."

When the bell rang signaling the end of class, Manuel started toward the door. Mike had anticipated this and stepped in the doorway. Manuel started to push to try to get around the student teacher, but Mike again ordered him back to his seat. As he started to retreat, his books sprawled onto the floor with papers flying everywhere. Manuel was "fighting mad" by this time. Given this condition, Mike wondered if he should continue to confront him now or let him go and deal with the problem later? He had to decide quickly, however, because Manuel was preparing for his second "charge."

### Becoming Involved

1. What procedure was Mike exposed to which is frequently used by students to justify themselves?

2. When teachers have students of different cultural backgrounds, there seems to be an increased tendency for problems. In what way(s) does this incident reflect this statement?

3. Was Mike wise in placing himself in a position which made him a physical "barrier" to Manuel?

### Field Exploration

Interview a teacher to determine how he convinces students that he is not prejudiced against them. Then interview some minority students and ask them which teacher of a different ethnic group they like best and why. At the next meeting attempt to formulate some guidelines concerning how you can best work with students from other cultures.

## Share and Tell Time

Mrs. Lewis believed that the educational system discriminated against her family because they lived in a housing project. Each of her children came to school demonstrating over contempt for teachers in general, and for Mrs. Howard in particular. Mrs. Lewis had frequently complained that Mrs. Howard had abused her children.

On the morning of the eleventh, the entire first floor of Hawthorne school was disturbed by a commotion in the hall. Mrs. Lewis was demanding to be taken to Mrs. Howard's room. When Mrs. Howard appeared in the hall, Mrs. Lewis screamed, "I am going to beat you up just like you did my Eddy."

Mrs. Howard gently affirmed, "I did not touch your child."

"Liar!" shrieked Mrs. Lewis. "You hit him yesterday at noon!"

Mrs. Howard called Eddy from the classroom and asked him what happened during the fight on the playground yesterday.

Eddy replied that she had taken hold of his shoulder and pulled him away while he was fighting with another boy."

Mrs. Lewis interrupted, menacingly, "Now Eddy, tell mother exactly what happened."

Eddy obediently replied to her demanding manner, "She hit me on the side of the head."

"There," she declared triumphantly, "You hit my boy."

Other teachers interrupted and prevented further confrontation by moving the gathering pupils back into their classrooms. Mrs. Lewis protestingly retreated into the school yard and eventually was persuaded to leave by officials who had been called to the scene.

Mrs. Howard began to restore order in her class and suggested that they might continue with their social dialogues. Several students participated and then Eddy raised his hand. Mrs. Howard was a bit startled, but she asked him what he would like to share. He rose from his seat, moved to the front of the room and announced to the class, "Mrs. Howard hit me on the side of the head."

### Becoming Involved

1. What is the probable origin of this confrontation?

2. Should the teacher have treated this incident differently than if it had been an accusation by a parent who reflected a middle class value system?

3. How should a teacher react toward other students following an embarrassing confrontation?

### Field Exploration

Elect a representative from within the class to make an appointment and visit a counselor or principal. Ask him to share with you the most memorable visit by a parent to his school. Was it made by a member of an ethnic group? Did it have any implications relating to the role of minorities?

## WHAT THE EXPERTS SAY

While much attention is given to meeting the needs of members of minority cultures, teachers often find themselves facing the dilemma of being keenly interested in serving minority students, but not knowing how to reach them. The following studies provide information which can be used to guide the teacher and adjust the classroom climate to reach this goal.

While not all multi-cultural groups are disruptive and uncooperative, teachers should be prepared to win over disinterested and boisterous classes. Sapp[2] observed a class of 30 racially balanced English grammar students in a predominately white rural high school in the Southeast. Each student, a lower to lower-middle class person, had been assigned to the class on the basis of prior poor performance. The supervising teacher described them as unconcerned, fidgety, unintelligent, uncooperative, overly talkative and the worst students in school. The rate of inappropriate behavior was inordinately high (75 percent).

During the second week, a class meeting was held for the students to discuss classroom problems. They said they had to be loud in order to be heard over their loud peers. The teacher suggested that one way to solve the problem might be to earn free time by engaging in the right kind of in-class behavior. The class was excited about the possibility of earning time to listen to records, talk to friends, and walk around the room.

A contract was drawn enabling students to earn five minutes of free time each day to use at the end of the week as they saw fit. Inappropriate behavior which required the teacher to stop the class and reprimand would result in loss of points. The students voted unanimously to accept the contract.

During the first week of the contract, the students' behavior had improved, so the teacher told them that they had behaved quite well and that she was sure that they would continue their good behavior even if the free time was no longer given. The contract was removed for one week, then reinstated to measure the difference in behavior.

The results were that the contract reduced the 75 percent level of bad behavior to 15 percent. Removal of the contract and

[2]G. L. Sapp & others. "Classroom Management & Student Involvement" *High School Journal* 56:276-83, Mr 73.

free time again produced a 75 percent level of misbehavior and when the contract was reinstated the misbehavior again declined to 15 percent.

What potential is there in using special reward systems on predominately black under-achievers in inner-city schools? A predominately black class of 20 juniors in an inner-city high school in the Southeast were underachievers and spent most of the period sleeping or talking.[3] The teacher used a discussion to lead the students to accept a point system rewarding good behavior. At the end of the period the points were converted into a grade. If a student gained enough points he could have ten minutes of free time at the end of the hour to listen to records, read comic books, or play games. In addition he could earn candy bars, bubble gum, participate in planning class activities, and contingent teacher attention. Initially, the teacher accepted almost any student comments. Later, the teacher reinforced self-referent statements and subject matter oriented statements.

The students began using more appropriate verbal expressions. They responded more to questions. On in-class study exercises they completed over 90 percent of them. The class average rose from "D" to "B" level. Students who had not shown interest in grades began checking and discussing their progress. The class attendance rose from 50 percent to 80 percent.

Exactly how can teachers provide for the needs of minority students? We often talk about providing for the needs of minority students, but do we really know what these needs are? The following are the recommendations of the National Association of Student Personnel Administration to be used by colleges to provide for needs of minority students.[4]

1. Encourage minority students to pursue challenges such as higher education.

2. Be flexible so that minority students can adjust their pace of development, if necessary, to your academic expectations and demands.

[3]Ibid
[4]National Association of Student Personnel Administration. *NASPA Journal*, 10:88-90, Oct., 1972.

3. Give special attention to the culture and heritage of minorities through social and cultural activities which involve all numbers.

4. Establish programs to provide for educational and social needs.

5. Develop procedures to assess academic areas in which they may need help. Prevent using standardized tests which do not account for the uniqueness of the experiences of minority students.

6. Establish an awareness program to acquaint other teachers and colleagues with the special needs of minorities.

7. Involve students in decision making.

8. Develop sensitivity toward problems and allow for diverse life styles.

9. Recruit and train qualified minority faculty and staff.

According to William Johnson, the problems which teachers have with low income and minority students is that they do not understand the terrible neighborhood, or home life of the students, or their peer group pressures.[5] Therefore, the teachers must educate themselves to the cultural, environmental, social, and economical plight of the ghetto youth. They must not give up. Then, they should help their fellow teachers to understand the ghetto.

Three conditions must exist if the teacher is to be successful with minority students:

1. The student must perceive congruence between his goals and the goals of his teacher.

2. The student must perceive that his teacher has the desire to help him attain these goals.

3. The student must perceive that his teacher has the ability to help him achieve his goals.

Exactly how shall we teach the culturally disadvantaged student? Proceeding on the definition of culturally disadvantaged as the products of a culture that has not provided them with the motivations, opportunities, experiences and relationships that will

[5]W. B. Johnson. "Misunderstanding Low Income and Minority Students" *Negro Education Review* 23:38-44, Jan. 1972.

enable their chances for competing successfully with their fellow citizens in all phases of life, Professor Bert O. Richmond[6] of the University of Georgia devised a classroom model for teachers of cultural minorities. He suggests that the classroom teacher approach each child as though he were unique (which, says Richmond, he is). The teacher should provide him opportunity to cooperate with his peers on assignments which will provide opportunity to understand and accept the limitations and strengths which he brings to the total effort.

The proposed model is the Peer Group Learning Unit having from six to eight members equated for sex, racial characteristics, and degree of cultural advantage. Each group should have a table and chairs spaced as far as possible from others in the room to use for self-understanding discussions. Some examples of appropriate exercises are:

1. What kind of person are you?
2. What behavior do you admire in people?
3. What are your interests?
4. What are your abilities?
5. In what ways is each person in this room unique?
6. What kind of person would you like to be?
7. What kind of behavior causes pupils to conflict with peers? parents? teachers?
8. Describe the kind of person you like best, least.

Richmond suggests that role playing, written exercises, group discussions, and art and music media be used in these exercises. A conflict with a peer (or parent) provides an excellent opportunity for students to try to understand another point of view and gain insight into the causes for human behavior. The group should be responsible for defining its own topics for exploration. Noise is to be tolerated.

It is not possible to effectively summarize the complexities involved in working with minority groups in a few short paragraphs.

[6]Bert O. Richmond, "Classroom Model for the Education of Cultural Minority Pupils" *Education* 92:8-12. F'72.

However, a few principles seem to emerge from the information provided in this section: 1. Students can often be reached if they are given more individual attention and rewards; 2. It is helpful to understand behavior in terms of how it originates from a minority culture; 3. One fruitful appraoch is to try to help individuals become more aware of themselves; and 4. A teacher may have to make some adjustments in standards and teaching style in order to reach minority students.

## DISCUSSION OF QUESTIONS

### The Phantom Strikes Twice

1. *What symbolic significance was there in the act of defacing pictures?* The incidents could represent a form of racism which completely rejects the contributions of someone from a different group.

2. *What evidence is there that some faculty members may be neglecting their responsibility in curbing this destruction?* Since the act was repeated on the very next day following its first commitment, it is possible that some teachers are not monitoring the school as closely as they might if minorities were defacing pictures of whites.

3. *As a teacher at Central, what could you do to help lessen the problem?* The act suggests that some students do not appreciate some of the significant contributions of minority leaders to this country or that their racial prejudices run deep. An open classroom discussion of both of these topics could prove helpful.

### Talk Only to Your Brother

1. *What evidence is there to suggest that the problem is racial?* Fred's explanation that he disliked being in school with whites; and the students' refusal to discuss the dismissal incident with a white teacher suggests that they were acutely aware of racial factors.

2. *How does this incident suggest that schools with black students should have black teachers?* Like any members of minority groups who bear aggressions toward the majority group, Fred and Jesse would probably view any restraining decision by a non-minority group member as prejudice against them.

3. *Was Mr. Kerlin's approach to this problem a wise one?* Mr. Kerlin chose this approach to let these students see their own prejudices. If they realize that their behavior may tend to perpetuate their problems, it may have been a good decision.

### Recipe for a Dropout

1. *What evidence is there that Mrs. Alexander is prejudiced against boys?* She apparently seems to apply a double standard in the class by criticizing the one male in the group.

2. *What behavior does Mark practice which suggests that his interest in cooking is diminishing?* Mark's test scores and lab grades have dropped to failing. His other teachers have indicated that he has become more passive. His increased class absences support his statement that "cooking is for girls. . .and if I have to continue the foods class, I'll quit school."

3. *This case describes apparent discrimination against a boy. What other examples of sex discrimination are practiced in the schools?* The most apparent illustration presently is the contention of girls that they are discriminated against in athletics.

### Manuel's Second Charge

1. *What procedure was Mike exposed to which is frequently used by students to justify themselves?* The accusation that he was being singled out and that the same criteria are not being applied to others.

2. *When teachers have students of different cultural backgrounds, there seems to be an increased tendency for problems. In what way(s) does this incident reflect this statement?* Manuel seemed to rationalize for all of his behavior by accusing the teacher of being prejudiced. It seems rather clear in this incident that little prejudice is reflected in the teacher's behavior, but in

177

many such schools the question of teacher prejudice is more real.

3. *Was Mike wise in placing himself in a position which made him a physical "barrier" for Manuel?* No. A teacher should try to avoid physical contact with a hostile student.

## Share and Tell Time

1. *What is the probable origin of this confrontation?* The most likely explanation may be that the involved parties had conflicting value systems; the teacher attempted to intervene in a conflict, and the mother perceived it as an attack upon her child and responded in anger.

2. *Should the teacher have treated this incident differently than if it had been an accusation by a parent who reflected a middle class value system?* Not necessarily. The teacher sought to remain calm and to control her emotions. This is a desired response whenever such confrontations occur, regardless of the parties involved.

3. *How should a teacher react toward his other students following an embarrassing confrontation?* Perhaps the best approach is to try to continue with composure because the students will likely appreciate the teacher's ability to remain calm in the presence of stress.

| | A G R E E | D I S A G R E E | U N D E C I D E D |
|---|---|---|---|

## POST-ASSESSMENT

### How do you feel?

1. Middle-class values are the standards by which school performance should be evaluated. — — —

2. The conflict of black and white values presents unmanageable tasks for the teacher when the groups are integrated. — — —

3. Teachers who work with minority-group pupils need specialized professional training. — — —

4. Any teacher who works with minorities must be prepared to cope with an additional syndrome of problems. — — —

5. The school is the best, and perhaps the only, institution which can provide the opportunity for divergent groups to get to know and understand each other. — — —

### What do you think?

1. The problem of minorities in the school encompasses any group which feels alienated because any majority tends to suppress the rights of a minority. — — —

2. Most racial incidents in schools are prompted by seemingly inocuous acts. — — —

3. Problems with minorities in schools often result from the lack of a relevant curriculum. — — —

4. The rights of the majority should take precedence over the demands of the minority. — — —

5. The typical school stresses conformity to its standards and has little tolerance for groups with differing views or goals. — — —

179

## SELF-ASSESSMENT

Now that you have completed the post-assessment, compare your pre- and post-assessment scores. Check those items where there is disagreement between responses. When possible, cite the specific reason which had some influence upon that change.

1. What did you learn about teaching minority groups?

2. What attitudes were examined or changed as a result of the analysis of minority group problems in the school?

3. What do you know and believe about:

   a. coping with minorities in schools?

   b. the specific needs of various minority groups?

   c. the variables that create friction with and among minority groups in education?

   d. discriminatory practices in education?

4. In your opinion, what are the principles which must be established in providing more effective education for minorities?

## FURTHER INVOLVEMENT

CARDENAS, R., and FILLMORE, L. W., "Toward a Multi-Cultural Society; Cultural Pluralism in the Schools," *Today's Education* 62:83-8, Spring, 1973.

This article focuses on assimilation of ethnic groups in the school. It particularly discusses the unique problems experienced by blacks. The article presents the point of view that multicultural education in the schools benefits all.

HENSON, K. T. "American Schools vs. Cultural Pluralism" *Educational Leadership*, 32:6, pp. 405-408, March, 1975.

Points out that members of minority groups should be understood, but should be expected to perform quality work in school. Views multi-cultural classes as opportunities to teach and learn about life in America.

AMERICAN ASSOCIATION OF COLLEGES FOR TEACHER EDUCATION, "Multicultural Education: Symposium," *Journal of Teacher Education* 24:262-308, Winter, 1973.

The entire issue of this journal presents a symposium on multicultural education. Choose your major interest and explore the thoughts of the experts.

RAMIREZ, HENRY M., "Multicultural Education to Make the Nation Greater," *NASSP Bulletin* 57:138-142, May, 1973.

Provides practical guidelines so that multicultural education can be instituted in the schools. Written mostly for administrators, this article may be used to see how the school actually views multicultural education.

SPRATLEN, THADDEUS, "Financing Inner City Schools; Policy Aspects of Economics, Political and Racial Disparity," *Journal of Negro Education* 42:283-307, Summer, 1973.

Shows the disparity of financing that exists in inner city schools. Does this affect the nature of education as you see it? Why or why not? What do you think of the author's proposals for reducing disparity, especially in the area of compensatory education?

# SECTION IV
# BECOMING INVOLVED IN
# THE SCHOOL COMMUNITY

# Chapter Ten

## ATHLETICS AND EXTRACURRICULAR ACTIVITIES

**PRE-ASSESSMENT**

|  | AGREEE | DISAGREEE | UNDECIDED |
|---|---|---|---|

*How do you feel?*

1. Extracurricular activities are generally more popular than any other aspect of a school program. — — —

2. Any teacher should cooperate with the school's extracurricular program even though it may be inconvenient at times. — — —

3. A coach should be selected on his ability to produce winners rather than his skill as a teacher. — — —

4. A well-rounded school program will provide opportunity for all students, male and female, to participate in some type of extraclass activities. — — —

5. Athletes are generally inferior academically to non-athletes. — — —

*What do you think?*

1. Extracurricular programs provide valuable recognition to students who otherwise would be unnoticed in the schools. — — —

2. Students learn as much from participating in extracurricular activities as they do from the content studied in the basic secondary school program. — — —

3. School social activities often produce desirable changes in the attitude of individual students. — — —

4. There is too much emphasis on athletics in the schools. — — —

5. Competition as intense as that displayed in athletics is basically detrimental to the individual personally and to the society collectively. — — —

## INTRODUCTION

A teacher's involvement with students extends far beyond the formal confines of the classroom. Extracurricular activities are as much an active, viable part of the school schedule as traditional studies. A look at a school is not complete without consideration of those activities that are school-related but are not actual formal areas of study. Here, students can individualize and perfect their skills in a more self-directed way. The recognition that may be denied or overlooked in the formal curriculum can sometimes be realized in one of the school's co-curricular functions. The activity program reflects a philosophy which advocates making the school more relevant and giving the individual an opportunity to shape his own course of events.

Athletics consume a major part of extracurricular time. Sports programs can provide solidarity for the school and frequently may give identity to an entire community. Many teachers, though, experience the frustration of seeing the "tail wag the dog," as athletic emphasis sometimes seems to preempt any systematic pursual of formal studies. The influence of athletics is shown as successful coaches seem to have the highest status and the athletic activities seem to be much more important than academic concerns. Some systems seem well entrenched with administrators who have blossomed from an athletic background and a community which frequently defines the quality of its school in terms of its success in the gymnasium or on the field.

The athletic world does have problems, though. The pressure to succeed presents many agonies for losing coaches. In addition, the women's movement is having a very real impact as equal rights in sports for all school people are being demanded. New problems and opportunities are presented by this development.

The extracurricular scene goes past athletics into many diverse kinds of programs, ranging from club activities to music and drama events. The teacher may sometimes feel that he does more teaching after school than he does during the school day as he works with students individually and helps them develop into more

184

mature individuals. Most teachers will quickly point out that they have really become acquainted with their pupils when they worked together in extracurricular concerns.

Involvement in extracurricular activities, like engrossment in all the other dimensions of teaching, presents dilemmas which must be dealt with in order for growth to continue. The following cases provide a few incidents which may confront the participant or new teacher. If you are aware of the possibilities and have considered some alternative courses of action, you should be more prepared to enter the extraclass world of the teacher.

## IN THE CLASSROOM
### School Ends At 3:30

Carla was an active, talented teacher-education major. Her college life was punctuated with sorority and social activities along with her formal studies. Her part-time job consumed an enormous amount of her spare time. It was difficult for her to arrange for the required field experiences which constituted her teaching program.

Once she was able to schedule her exploratory activities, she found that she was very much in demand by the school. When it was discovered that she was a former cheerleader and a rather creative person overall, she was asked to remain after school to help with various activities. Although her supervisors explained that any teacher should get to know what school is like by participating in the extracurricular program, she actually thought that she was being exploited because she had some talents to contribute and since the teachers seemed to be overworked.

She was at the point where she had to make some decisions. Was it so important for her to participate in additional school functions that she should reduce her college activities and curtail the hours which she spent on her part-time job? "Is it so necessary to participate in after-school activities,?" she asked, "After all school ends at 3:30, and I understand what is happening there during the day."

185

## Becoming Involved

1. What seems to be the message which the teachers are communicating?

2. If a teaching candidate feels exploited during his field experiences, how can he determine the validity of his feelings and seek assistance?

3. What are some reasons which would support the case to have a student become involved in extracurricular activities?

## Field Exploration

Attend a few extracurricular activities (dances, parties, music activities, etc.). What types of responsibilities are demanded of teachers? What kinds of teaching skills are needed to work with students in the extracurricular program? What do you notice about the students who are participating?

### You Won't Report This Incident

South Antioch fully supports the athletic program at the local high school. School pride is manifested through the box scores instead of the academic education of the school. The people in the community seem almost to idolize Roger Gord, who has coached six successful football seasons.

Mr. Gord's ability and desire to be a good teacher fall far short of his zeal to be a good football coach. He has little overt interest in his classes, and he frequently reports to the classroom fifteen to twenty minutes late. The love of football has precluded anyone complaining about his professional demeanor. The principal, who initiated football at the school and hired Gord six years ago, is prone to support the coach on the basis of his successful record.

This year, Alan May, a bright young man who was active in enhancing the image of the teaching profession, was appointed as a new teacher at South Antioch. Although he is interested in athletics, he was dismayed at the coach's privileges, his attitude toward teaching, and his indifference to his classes. He grew more disturbed as the year progressed. One day, as he unexpectedly stopped by the coach's office, he saw several empty beer bottles in the trash can. He stood unnoticed as Mr. Gord began to dispose of them by placing them in a laundry bag. As Alan shuffled his feet, the coach became aware of his presence, started toward him, stopped, and then began talking.

Slowly but carefully Gord admonished, "I know you will not report this incident to anyone. No one will accept your word over mine."

Mr. May said nothing, but he left the area wondering whether any action would be taken in regard to Gord's behavior even if they believed his report.

### Becoming Involved

1. What weaknesses or undesirable qualities did Coach Gord display?

2. What conditions suggest that Alan's account of the incident would not have been accepted?

3. Does Coach Gord's success in any way excuse his drinking?

4. Does his success as a coach compensate for his lack of classroom effectiveness?

### Field Exploration

Talk with coaches and teachers and ask which criteria are used to evaluate a coach—his team's record or his teaching? Visit classes taught by coaches and non-coaches in the same subject area. Are there any apparent differences in their classroom instructional patterns?

## The Girls Are In Our Gym

The gymnasium was a male sanctuary at Webster High School. The girls could use the facility only during the late evening hours or at some other inconvenient time when the male teams were not practicing. Since there were many varsity and reserve teams, the facility was usually occupied by the boys.

Barb Hendricks came onto the scene as a challenger to male supremacy in the athletic program. As an ambitious, active physical education major, she intended to secure more benefits and privileges for the girls at the school. Using recent federal legislation as her authority, she generated support for equality of funds, an increase in the number of girls' teams and coaches, and parity in the use of facilities.

The obvious tension developed with members of the male coaching staff. They cited the fact that shared revenue would jeopardize the entire athletic program. If they did not have the money to adequately support a team, there would be no revenue for anyone. This means that the boys must have sufficient funding as well as a generous amount of practice time. They pointed out that girls' teams should be self-supporting if they were to exist and not depend on the funds from the established program. They were convinced that if Barb had her way, there would be no program for anyone at the school in a few years.

Barb countered with the fact that not all support comes from revenue accrued at athletic contests. She further challenged the coaches to prove that successful athletics for a few were more beneficial than participation by many. She continued to press for her demands and was supported by women's groups, civil rights groups, and federal guidelines.

The confrontation emerged one Thursday after school when the girls' basketball team occupied the gymnasium while the coach was having a strategy session with his boys in the locker room. When they emerged to practice, Barb refused to yield the floor to the agitated coach. She did offer to let them use half of the gymnasium, suggesting that the boys could have the entire floor at 6:00, when she planned to finish her practice.

### Becoming Involved

1. What gave Barb Hendricks the impetus to challenge male supremacy?

2. The coach made at least one point which is difficult to refute. What was it?

3. What are the basic issues for teachers in this conflict?

### Field Exploration

What is the status of girls' athletics in the schools? Talk with a woman coach and with a male coach and secure their reactions. Are guidelines being developed so that the girls' and boys' teams can work together harmoniously? Are there some new opportunities developing for females in this area? What type of preparation is needed?

If possible, try to discern the amount of funds presently appropriated for girls' and boys' athletic programs. Are there any changes in this area?

It might also be interesting to obtain a practice schedule. Who makes maximum use of the facilities?

## We Lost the Game

Tension reached its peak at Jackson High School during the fifth period. The strain had been increasing all day because the basketball squad had lost its preliminary tournament game for the first time in years. The situation was complicated when a few students from the winning school (which had dismissed classes for the day) appeared outside to taunt the students at Jackson. A few minor fights had broken out and tension was high.

It was in this environment that Miss Paul attempted to begin teaching her senior speech class. Her problems were compounded by the fact that the leading scorer for the basketball team and the captain of the cheerleading squad were both members of the class along with Adam, a small student who frequently clashed with athletes. Since he had tried out and failed to make the football, basketball, and baseball teams, he had become antagonistic toward all sports and participants.

Miss Paul decided that she could not immediately launch into her planned discussion of parliamentary procedure so she guided the students in random discussion, hoping to later focus on the planned topic. Inevitably the conversation led to the basketball game, and some spirited conversation ensued. Eventually, Miss Paul realized her opportunity to move to the discussion of parliamentary procedure, and she began to write a few notes on the chalkboard.

As her back was turned, she heard Dale, a basketball player, utter a threat; she turned and noticed that Collene, a cheerleader, was in tears and Dale was confronting Adam. Apparently Adam had made some comment about the game to them.

Miss Paul told them to stop, but Adam continued with a few pointed remarks. She finally regained control by threatening to take punitive action; however, Adam sat quietly and stared sullenly at her. "All of this because the team lost a game," she thought.

### Becoming Involved

1. What were some obvious clues that the students were pre-occupied with athletics?

2. What is the meaning behind Adam's taunts?

3. Was Miss Paul's attempt to divert the student's attention from the ballgame a wise one?

### Field Exploration

Attend one of the "important" athletic contests at a local school and sit in the fan section if possible. How do people feel about the contest? Then visit the school and observe some of the better athletes in their classes. How are they treated? Do you see any Adams in the room?

## Another Successful Year

Pam Brooks was impressed with the initiation of the school year. Since she was an English teacher, she was encouraged by the fact that the principal, a former coach, seemed to show sincere interest in her department. His comments seemed to indicate that he had a very comprehensive philosophy of education.

After the initial period of excitement, though, Pam became bewildered by a series of events which occurred in the ensuing weeks. With the beginning of the football season, Pam's classes

190

were continuously disrupted by announcements on the intercom. Student assistants brought notices saying first one, then another player was to report to the coach's office. Eventually, daily written announcements included a list of students who were to be excused for football practice. The attendance in her senior English class decreased thirty percent on these occasions.

"This is absurd," she thought. "Something has to be done."

She talked with some of the other teachers, but they merely dismissed the inconvenience as another "necessary evil" of teaching. She was tired of the phrase and could not understand why the teachers were so complacent about it. They merely smiled when she suggested that the principal be approached.

The team continued to go undefeated. It was almost impossible to shop in town whenever the team was playing, because the stores closed and the merchants went to the game. The conversation in the community seemed inevitably to get around to the contest of the week. The whole town appeared to be engrossed in the team's accomplishments.

It became more apparent to Miss Brooks that this was an athletic-dominated school and that the principal was really the team's number-one fan. His professional demeanor began to diminish as the team soared and she became disillusioned about the priorities of the principal and the community.

### Becoming Involved

1. Was Pam Brooks' initial impression of the principal invalid?
2. Why would a principal be so concerned with sports?
3. What could a teacher do to bring athletics back into proper perspective?

### Field Exploration

If you have time, survey the secondary principals in the area. How many of them have experience in athletics? How much of a principal's time is consumed by athletic affairs? How important are athletics to the school in comparison to the other curricular and extracurricular activities?

## Ryder's Track Team

Fifty yards from the finish, Ray Zurich was fighting the top man for the lead; forty yards, they were side by side; thirty yards, Ray had a half step lead. Twenty yards; ten yards; five. Ray crossed the finish line two steps ahead of his arch rival, Terry Bishop of Grover High School. What a finish and what a track season it would be for Ryder High School! Coach Pete Bryant had been building for this season since Ray and his fellow athletes were freshmen. Now that they were seniors, strong and anxious to win, the thought of a possible conference victory was more than a mere desire in the coach's mind.

Ray was one of the key persons on the team because he was an all-around performer. The coach was confident that he and his fellow seniors could amass enough points to bring a conference championship to the school. He was fantasizing about such an accomplishment when the homeward-bound bus bumped to a halt with a flat tire.

As the wait for help grew longer the boys became impatient. Ray had plans for the evening and he began to discuss his plight with his best friend, Ron. Ray suggested that they hitchhike back to school. Ron agreed, and the two boys stole away. Their absence was not discovered until the bus arrived back at school several hours later.

Coach Bryant called the two athletes to his office on Monday. He told them that he had been very concerned with their safety and their whereabouts and then he suspended both boys from the team temporarily. This meant that they would not be able to participate in the Taylor Relays, the most important event prior to the championship events.

Ray had waited the whole year for this next meet. He was sure of victory and it was the meet in which the coveted Taylor Trophies were awarded annually to those winning two or more events. He said to Coach Bryant, "I can't let you suspend me; I want to run in the next meet." Mr. Bryant calmly told Ray he had no choice. Putting everything on the line for something he wanted very badly Ray said, "If I can't run this meet, I'll never run again, and very frankly you need me to win the conference championship."

Coach Bryant had committed himself. If he decided to concede and let Ray compete in the meet, this would be a poor example to the other boys. Was it possible that his penalty was too severe? Could he retract what he had been emphasizing about strict discipline and character building? On the other hand, this season was so important to the team as well as its director. Coach Bryant had a very important decision to make.

### Becoming Involved

1. What reasons would Coach Bryant have for suspending Ray?

2. What forces were impelling him to excuse Ray?

3. What judgmental errors were made by the coach?

4. What alternatives would save the team's destiny and yet help to preserve Coach Bryant's professional status?

### Field Exploration

For the sake of both the academic and athletic programs of any school no athlete should ever be considered indispensable. Single out one of the more athletic oriented class members to talk to the class during the next meeting. There will be two objectives: first, to explain why an athletic "king" is potentially dangerous (a) to the athletic program and (b) to the academic curriculum.

Any coaching majors in the class might wish to talk to a coach and to a few selected athletes to determine how rules are made and enforced.

## The Rehearsal

The annual Bryan Review was a highlight at Bryan High School. The elaborate production featured thoroughly-rehearsed, creative entertainment provided by the school's talented students. The planning began early in the school year and culminated with the spring production.

193

In order for the performance to be successful, there had to be several evening rehearsals involving the entire cast. The presence of nearly one hundred persons often created supervisory problems for the sponsoring teachers. Although the normal rules were espoused (no one outside the cast allowed in the building, all students stay on the main floor, no smoking, pay attention to the director, etc.,), it was difficult to effectively organize so that the students were not wasting time.

At Tuesday's practice the group seemed in a more spirited mood than usual. Several girls were engaged in some kind of impromptu game at the far end of the gym; other students were away from their posts when they were supposed to be on cue; lines were forgotten, and there were a couple of arguments between the girls in the junior choir. The two-and one-half hour practice period seemed to drone on and on with no apparent end.

The sponsoring teachers were irritated by the lack of progress and concerned that such little improvement was being made. Was it worth all the effort? Would the students be ready to perform? How can we get the students to take their responsibilities more seriously when we cannot exert the same techniques that we would use in a class?

### Becoming Involved

1. How can an activity such as the review be justified as a valid school activity?

2. What could the student behavior symbolize?

3. What can teachers do in order to modify such a situation?

### Field Exploration

Ask to participate in working with some extraclass activity and, if possible, secure some independent responsibility. How do the students respond to your suggestions? What works? What does not work?

### WHAT THE EXPERTS SAY

No one acquainted with educational practices today would question the important place which is being filled by student activities outside the classroom. The aims of education can often be achieved in the school activities program when they are not possible in the regular school curriculum. The role of the teacher involves some responsibilities beyond classroom teaching.[1] Often, one of these additional responsibilities is sponsoring and advising formal and informal student organizations.

What are the benefits which result from this involved participation which frequently extends into the evening and week-end hours? According to Bent and Unruh,[2] there are several values. Activities provide experiences which are not otherwise available, permitting students to make applications of knowledge acquired in various courses. The cocurricular activities make it possible to offer a well-rounded, balanced program including intellectual, physical, social, and emotional experiences that provide an excellent learning climate. Such experiences sometimes also approximate life in the adult community and provide preparation for the roles the student will eventually play in adult life. It has been shown, too, that activities have increased the holding power of secondary schools.

The extracurricular schedule, like the rest of the curriculum, reflects the changes that occur in the school's program. According to Buser[3] who studied extracurricular trends, activities which have been added appeared to be organizations that were oriented toward increased student involvement in the pressing problems of society, including such activities as ecology clubs, black culture societies and women's liberation clubs. Popularity was also expressed for leisure-oriented clubs, school-community service groups, governance activities (faculty advisory board, student senate, etc.), and interscholastic athletics. Activities such as subject-related clubs (math, science, language), hobby, school dances, and pep clubs seemed to have declined in popularity.

The experts seem to indicate that the extracurricular program

[1]National Association of Secondary School Principals, "The Student Activities Program," *Bulletin of NASSP*, January, 1971, p. 63.

[2]Rudyard K. Bent, and Adolph Unruh, *Secondary School Curriculum*, D. C. Heath and Co., Lexington, MA, pp. 134-138.

[3]Robert L. Buser, "What's Happening in Student Activities in the Schools of the Seventies?" *NASSP Bulletin*, September, 1971, pp. 1-9.

195

is more entrenched in the school curriculum than it has ever been, and it is still growing. Philosophically and scientifically, it appears to be justified as a valid endeavor. Teachers will find themselves involved in some aspect of student activity.

No other country accords athletics as much attention in the school curriculum as the American schools. Yet, no other country even claims to attempt to educate the masses of its population. The two goals may seem to conflict, but does athletics really affect academic achievement? If so, how, and to what degree? The following reports represent a good sampling of the findings and opinions of the experts.

Our first question might be, "are athletes inferior academically to non-athletic students?" Several studies have shown that the answer is no, according to the findings of Schafer[4] who says, "athletes are not inferior," and another report by Eidsmore[5] whose study indicates that "high school athletes are brighter."

The work of another expert, Elmer Spreitzer,[6] extends beyond these studies in an attempt to discover why athletes are better students than non-athletes. Spreitzer explains that "sports involvement tends to engender high perceived peer status which in turn stimulates a desire for further status acquisition." He hastens to point out that athletics has this motivating effect only in schools where interscholastic achievement is valued highly relative to scholarly achievement. But he also adds that "athletic participation increases academic motivation irrespective of student grade average, socio-economic status, parental encouragement, and measured I.Q."

Does this stimulating influence carry on into college? Yes, according to Bend[7] who found that athletes have high educational

[4]W. E. Schafer, "Athletes are Not Inferior Students." *Transaction* November, 1968, pp. 21-26, 61-62.

[5]R. M. Eidsmore, "High School Athletes are Brighter." *School Activities* 35: November, 1963, pp. 75-77.

[6]Elmer Spreitzer and M. Pugh, "Interscholastic Athletics and Educational Expectations." *Sociology of Education,* 46: Spring, 1973, pp. 171-82.

[7]E. Bend "The Impact of Athletic Participation on Academic and Career Aspiration and Achievement." *The National Football Foundation Hall of Fame:* New Brunswick, N.J., 1968.

expectations and higher rates of college attendance than their non-athletic counterparts.

But, perhaps we should ask another question which extends even further. In what other ways are athletes different? Schendal[8] found that athletes differ in several ways from non-athletic students. "Athletes tend to be more extroverted, conventional in life style, positive in self-concepts, and have lower rates of delinquency than non-athletes."

Like non-athletic students, not all athletes are academically inclined. Therefore a question should be asked to help teachers work with athletes, "how can the non-academically inclined athlete be motivated?" In 1973, Sapp[9] conducted a study to learn whether freedom can be used to motivate non-academically inclined athletes. A senior English class of seventeen male, middle-class athletes who were enthusiastic about athletics, but not academics, were working slowly, requiring as long as 63 days to complete a chapter and averaging "C-" on a series of tests.

Then the teacher began allowing students to go to the library to complete their assignments. If they completed five pages correctly they could go to the library to pursue their own interests. After a week, further restrictions were added: each sentence and paragraph construction was to become smoother and more coherent. The athletes talked more positively about the class, the time required to finish the chapter decreased to four days, and the class average rose to "B+". In essence, the students were spending half as much time in class and doing three times as much work.

One of the most active arenas for extracurricular activities today is in the area of athletics for girls. The elimination of sex discrimination in sports as dictated by Title IX of the Education Amendments of 1972 forbids discrimination based on sex in any educational program or activity receiving federal funds. Since virtually every public school in the nation receives some kind of federal assistance, the order is binding on the schools. Conse-

---

[8]J. Schendal, "Psychological Differences Between Athletes and Non-Participants at three Educational Levels." *Research Quarterly.* 36: March, 1965, pp. 52-67.

[9]Gary L. Sapp, and others, "Classroom Management and Student Involvement." *High School Journal.* Vol. 56, No. 6, March, 1973, pp. 279.

quently, the schools are having to justify their programs on the basis that they do not discriminate.

Section 86.41(c) of Title IX requires equal opportunity in athletic programs for men and women. Those who have studied the legislation indicate that there are specific factors which should be used by an educational institution during its self-evaluative planning to determine whether equal opportunity exists in its plan for its total athletic program. The following are specifically mentioned:

*The nature and extent of the sports programs to be offered (including the levels of competition, such as varsity, club, etc.)

*The provision of equipment and supplies.

*The scheduling of games and practice time.

*The provision of travel and per diem allowances.

*The nature and extent of the opportunity to receive coaching and academic tutoring.

*The assignment and compensation of coaches and tutors.

*The provision of locker rooms, practice and competitive facilities.

*The provision of housing and dining facilities and services.

*The nature and extent of publicity.

The experts seem to agree that the point of the regulation is to see that each sex has an equal opportunity to compete in athletics in a meaningful way. Obviously there will be considerable changes in the structure of the schools' athletic programs in the next few years. In all probability, they will provide increased participation for a greater number of people.

These studies have provided answers to some important concerns. However, other questions still remain unanswered such as; What effects do athletic programs have on non-athletic students? Do the positive effects of athletics upon parents and other community members outweigh the damage that is often incurred upon school and community rapport?

This information suggests that we as teachers should be aware of our generalizations about athletics and should rid ourselves of those pre-set stereotypes for which we have no support. It also implies that when working with athletes we should begin by assuming that they are interested and capable, and when we find otherwise we should use positive approaches, involving these students in establishing working guidelines and in planning curriculum activities for them.

## DISCUSSION OF QUESTIONS

### School Ends At 3:30

1. *What seems to be the message which the teachers are communicating?* Professionals are needed after school as well as during the regular school hours, and a person does not see a total school experience unless he is aware of what transpires in the extracurricular program.

2. *If a teaching candidate feels exploited during his field experiences, how can he determine the validity of his feelings and seek assistance?* He should examine the nature of the assigned tasks. Do they go beyond merely providing assistance for a busy teacher, i.e., what is there to learn from the participation? If he feels exploited, he should contact a responsible person at the university and explain his feelings.

3. *What are some reasons which would support the case to have a student become involved in extracurricular activities?* Teachers and teaching candidates get to know students better through informal participation in extraclass activities. This kind of activity also allows a teaching candidate to contribute any unique talents or skills which he may possess. In addition, it gives him more visibility so that school personnel will know him better.

### You Won't Report This Incident

1. *What weaknesses or undesirable qualities did Coach Gord display?* He showed little interest in his teaching and frequently was late to class. He was untidy in his appearance and apparently had been drinking at school.

2. *What conditions suggest that Alan's account of the inci-*

199

*dent would not have been accepted?* Alan is a new teacher at South Antioch; Coach Gord is not. The coach has a six-year record of winning at a school where there is more pride in athletics than in academics.

3. *Does Coach Gord's success in any way excuse his drinking?* No. It must not, because the coach, like any teacher, is responsible for the moral image he presents to his students. Even though he feels that it is all right, he must respect the values of many of his students and their parents who may think otherwise.

4. *Does his success as a coach compensate for his lack of classroom effectiveness?* No. In the classroom students need academic guidance. By his failure to teach effectively, Coach Gord was cheating these students of this leadership.

## The Girls Are In Our Gym

1. *What gave Barb Hendricks the impetus to challenge male supremacy?* Undoubtedly the basic support has originated in the women's movement in general. Then, too, one has to recognize the strength of Barb's convictions and her courage in challenging a sacred institution. Thirdly, she has some actual support in the recent government regulations barring sex discrimination in athletics (Title IX).

2. *The coach made at least one point which is difficult to refute. What was it?* Although he may have overstated the case, it is common knowledge that the revenue from the popular sports often provides at least some funds for the less-popular programs.

3. *What are the basic issues for teachers in this conflict?* The following issues need to be recognized: the question of how athletics should be supported; the nature or priorities for males and females in the use of facilities and the expenditure of funds; the meaning of equality; and, ultimately, an examination of the merit of producing a team that is likely to win vs. the merit of providing an opportunity for more students to participate in athletic activities.

## We Lost the Game

1. *What were some obvious clues that the students were pre-occupied with athletics?* The students turned the random discussion into talk about the game, and the athlete and cheerleader were defensive as the result of a few gibes from another student.

2. *What is the meaning behind Adam's taunts?* It conveys the symbolic message that a person may be important and effective even though he is not an athlete. It also implies that athletics are over-emphasized in schools.

3. *Was Miss Paul's attempt to divert the student's attention from the ballgame a wise one?* Probably so. Although the feelings were strong, a teacher must convey the message that athletics constitute just one phase of a school program and that the present class has objectives to be met.

## Another Successful Year

1. *Was Pam Brooks' initial impression of the principal invalid?* Although the case might appear to point to that conclusion, there is the possibility that the principal may provide leadership more in keeping with his philosophy as the year progresses. In order to answer this question, one needs to know how much attention is given to curriculum and how much support the faculty receives.

2. *Why would a principal be so concerned with sports?* A successful principal must always be aware of the desires of the community. If he were not sensitive to athletics, he would soon be out of favor in the community. Since he was a former coach, he naturally would have a lively interest in the team.

3. *What could a teacher do to bring athletics back into proper perspective?* One possibility might be to unite with other teachers to develop the academic program so that its progress would also capture the attention and support of the community.

## Ryder's Track Team

1. *What reasons would Coach Bryant have for suspending Ray?* Ray knowingly violated a school rule, one which is necessary

for providing safety for the team members. It might encourage Ray and his peers to ignore other regulations if an exception were made in this case.

2. *What forces were impelling him to excuse Ray?* Ray's lack of participation would destroy any opportunity to win the conference championship which the coach coveted.

3. *What judgmental errors were made by the coach?* He made a unilateral decision, and he failed to recognize that the boys might resist his disciplinary procedure. He made an arbitrary statement which left no apparent recourse to the students except to withdraw.

4. *What alternatives would save the team's destiny and yet help to preserve Coach Bryant's professional status?* Coach Bryant could offer some type of alternative disciplinary procedure.

## The Rehearsal

1. *How can an activity such as the Review be justified as a valid school activity?* It promotes school spirit and provides an opportunity for many students to display individual talent. An activity such as this is also an experiment in working together where a person has to assume some individual responsibility in order for the effort to be a success.

2. *What could the student behavior symbolize?* The overt behavior may initially appear to be indifference or immaturity. Although that may be true, it may indicate that the students are anxious and insecure. The behaviors may mean that they are seeking comfortable ways of dealing with their apprehensive feelings about the production.

3. *What can teachers do in order to modify such a situation?* First, perhaps, they should examine their organizational structure to see if it can be improved. Have there been inconsistencies or obscure instructions? Secondly, teachers may want to practice more positive reinforcement of performance so that students will feel better about what they are doing and be less threatened in their rehearsals.

## POST-ASSESSMENT

| | A G R E E E | D I S A G R E E E | U N D E C I D E D |
|---|---|---|---|

### How do you feel?

1. Extracurricular activities are generally more popular than any other aspect of a school program. __ __ __

2. Any teacher should cooperate with the school's extracurricular program even though it may be inconvenient at times. __ __ __

3. A coach should be selected on his ability to produce winners rather than his skill as a teacher. __ __ __

4. A well-rounded school program will provide opportunity for all students, male and female, to participate in some type of extraclass activities. __ __ __

5. Athletes are generally inferior academically to non-athletes. __ __ __

### What do you think?

1. Extracurricular programs provide valuable recognition to students who otherwise would be unnoticed in the schools. __ __ __

2. Students learn as much from participating in extracurricular activities as they do from the content studied in the basic secondary school program. __ __ __

3. School social activities often produce desirable changes in the attitude of individual students. __ __ __

4. There is too much emphasis on athletics in the schools. __ __ __

5. Competition as intense as that displayed in athletics is basically detrimental to the individual personally and to the society collectively. __ __ __

203

## SELF-ASSESSMENT

Now that you have completed the post-assessment, compare your pre- and post-assessment scores. Check those items where there is disagreement between responses. When possible, cite the specific factors that had some influence on that change.

1. Should an athletic program receive as much emphasis and support as the school's academic program?

2. What should a teacher do if he feels that the emphasis on extracurricular activities is proving to be detrimental to the successful progress of his class?

3. Schools are often run according to the athletic philosophy (competition, survival of the fittest, rigid control from the top, etc.). Do you feel that this style is superior to one which is more democratic and flexible?

4. Would you ever fail an athlete when you knew that it would deny him the opportunity to display his best skill through participation in sports?

## FURTHER INVOLVEMENT

AMERICAN SCHOOL BOARD, "Schoolgirl Athletes Are Shaking Things Up," *American School Board Journal* 160:9, pp. 23-25, Sep., 1973.

Describes instances of participation by girls on traditionally all male sports teams.

ELAM, STANLEY, "Athletics and Education: Are They Compatible?" *Phi Delta Kappan* 56:2, October, 1974.

The entire issue of the journal is devoted to the topic of athletics and education. Several articles focus on the involvement of secondary schools. Many different points of view are considered. Two articles, "The Sixty Game Winning Streak: Who Won? Who Lost?," and "The Values of Athletics in Schools: A Continuous Debate," should provide plenty of background for discussion and exploration.

MONAHAN, DAN, "Stimulating Interest in World History Through Simulation Baseball," *Education* 94:2, pp. 175-76, Nov./Dec., 1973.

Discusses an instructional method for stimulating student interest in learning world history.

NOLTE, CHESTER M., "With Prodding from Girls (and Courts), Public Schools Are Backing Away from Sex Bias in Physical Education Programs," *American School Board Journal* 160:9, pp. 20-23, September, 1973.

Examines some recent court cases involving sex discrimination in school athletic events and discusses the implications these cases could hold collectively as far as public schools are concerned.

WOODER, GARY, "How Not to Let the Sports Tail Wag the Education Dog," *American School Board Journal* 160:21-23, August, 1972.

This will not be the coach's favorite article. It states that inter-scholastic sports are costing districts the best possible physical education programs, the best intramural sports program, and best possible athletic programs for girls. Read it, and then strike up a discussion with that acquaintance of yours who wants to be a coach.

## Chapter Eleven

# THE TEACHER AND THE COMMUNITY

| | **AGREE** | **DISAGREE** | **UNDECIDED** |
|---|---|---|---|

## PRE-ASSESSMENT

### *How Do You Feel?*

1. The relationship of the teacher to the community should be similar to that of an employee to an employer. — — —

2. Ultimately a teacher should obey his own professional conscience rather than submit to community pressure. — — —

3. Controversial reading material should be included in the curriculum if it has value, even though there may be parental objection. — — —

4. The school should be a lamp not a mirror, i.e. it should lead the community rather than reflect it. — — —

5. A teacher should comply with the demands of the community only in sensitive curriculum areas like sex education. — — —

### *What Do You Think?*

1. The most frequent cause of difficulties between teacher and community relates to curriculum. — — —

2. School officials must learn to interpret the true needs of the community and find ways of fulfilling them. — — —

3. Teachers must satisfy the requests of parents even when their desires seem unreasonable. — — —

4. When the board of trustees uses poor judgment which results in potential damage to the school program, teachers are obligated to react. — — —

5. Community feelings are usually so diverse that there is no way that a teacher can actually be aware of prevailing views. — — —

## INTRODUCTION

The school was created by the community and is supported by the community; therefore, the teachers should obey the public at large when it gives directions. Or is the school a specialized institution composed of professional people who should not be controlled by laymen but who should use their own expertise to make their own decisions?

American schools are servants of society. In the simplest form, public schools are just that--public. They belong to the people and exist as institutions serving them. This means that the patrons decide on what they want from the schools. They establish the objectives and policies, delegate to the professionals the responsibility for implementing these policies, and reserve for themselves the role of accountant by evaluating the results.[1]

Although the school reflects the needs and desires of the local population, there are many who feel that it should provide leadership for society. Public education deals with a range of objectives which focus on leadership: preparing everyone for full participation in a free and open society; equipping each person with intellectual and emotional tools to survive in a post-industrial environment; equalizing opportunities for all children; and preparing children to cope with the dynamic nature of today's world.

Sometimes the objectives of the community and those of the school seem to be in conflict. This creates frustration for both parties. Some citizens may monitor the learning program to see that no alien ideas enter. The teachers may perceive such moves to be menacing unless they understand the reasons for various actions and can effectively counteract them.

The following cases represent incidents which, when seen through teachers' eyes, indicate that some citizens are trying to modify the school program to conform to their desires. Can you analyze the basic problems that exist and determine what future teachers need to know and do in order to work effectively with the community and its representatives instead of feeling threatened by it?

[1]Mario Fantini, *The People and Their Schools: Community Participation*, Phi Delta Kappa Fastback No. 62, Bloomington, IN, 1975, p. 8.

# IN THE CLASSROOM
## The Rise and Fall of Mr. Dukes

When Mr. Dukes, a teacher from an upper-middle-class background, moved to Lakeland High School, he introduced some economics classes which had not been previously available. Although his classes were considered to be very demanding, they were designed to be beneficial for those who were contemplating higher education.

Since many of his students were college bound, he conducted each class like a university course. He lectured or simply talked about problems and ways to handle them. Outside readings were expected with only essay tests for evaluation.

The students were not quite prepared for this approach and had difficulty understanding him. They criticized his opinions which seemed to be opposed to the prevailing values in the area. The number of complaints increased as student resentment of his views and his teaching methods grew. The rumor soon spread that he was openly challenging our present economic system. Complaints were received from within the school and from the community. The criticisms progressively became more personal and more bitter although he purported to ignore them. Ultimately, he was subjected to threatening and abusive phone calls as well as vandalism of his classroom. Mr. Dukes attempted to remain composed, but these accusations and assaults were beginning to produce considerable stress.

### Becoming Involved

1. What do you know about Mr. Dukes' students which gives support to his teaching techniques?

2. Why was Mr. Dukes harassed by the community at large?

3. Should a teacher be permitted to select his own preferred teaching style?

4. Should the community be permitted to impose its values on Mr. Dukes' way of teaching?

### Field Exploration

Prepare a questionnaire and mail it to randomly selected

citizens. Prepare questions which will permit them to describe what they think of teachers. Are they suspicious of what is being taught? What would they do if a teacher were allegedly teaching something which is contrary to their views?

## Open Discussion of a Closed Topic

Mrs. Marshall checked attendance in her co-educational family living class and initiated conversation designed to lead to a discussion of planning a family budget. Stacy, the most outspoken student in the room, politely stated that she was not concerned about family finance yet since she is going to college and knows that it will be some time before she is concerned with home money management. She indicated that she wanted to discuss ideas which were more closely related to her now. The class echoed her wish, and Mrs. Marshall asked them what subject they felt was relevant. There was a chorus of requests to discuss pre-marital sex.

Realizing that in this conservative community this subject could easily lead to misunderstanding, Mrs. Marshall was tempted to veto the idea. However, this class had been hard to reach, so she decided that she would not lose this opportunity to establish communication. She had always felt that the family living class should be one in which the students could discuss problems of concern to them, so she agreed that premarital sex would be the topic for the day.

The discussion was quite lively and almost everyone participated. Students were beginning to express their ideas and to analyze a closed topic. During the session, one of the girls asked the teacher's opinion on whether or not it was the girl who had everything to lose in premarital sex experiences because she was the one who had to worry about becoming pregnant. Mrs. Marshall replied that pregnancy was not as likely to be such a compelling concern now that dependable birth control devices are available. She went on to explain that the real danger was in the area of mental repercussions. She asked, "Will you be plagued

209

with guilt feelings and can you handle them?" The bell sounded and a couple of girls admitted that they had never before thought about that implication. The students filed out of the room, and Mrs. Marshall was confident that a difficult, sensitive topic had been candidly discussed.

The next morning in the teachers' lounge, Mr. Watson asked her what had happened in the family living class to cause such a disturbance. Mrs. Marshall was puzzled and asked him to explain. The women at the auxiliary meeting, it seems, were discussing what their children had been told in class. It was reported that Mrs. Marshall remarked that premarital sex was all right as long as one does not feel that it is wrong.

Mrs. Marshall was astonished. She had grown up in this community and she felt that this could not happen to her. She had been wrongly accused, but how could she present her defense? She knew that the principal would support her if objections were raised, but she was also aware that if the parents acted in consort (and this was quite possible), they would not permit their children to enroll in any of her elective classes. How could she convince the parents that the class was beneficial and that her comments were reported out of context?

### Becoming Involved

1. Can the study of premarital sex in this class be justified?

2. What was the real basis for Mrs. Marshall's problem?

3. Suppose that you are a fellow teacher at this school, and Mrs. Marshall comes to you for advice. What suggestions can you offer?

### Field Exploration

Problems between teachers and parents often originate because of poor communications. Talk with some parents of teenagers. Ask them what kinds of contacts they have with the teachers. Ask them if they are invited to the school and, if so, how often and for what occasions.

### It Said, "Damn"

The following story appeared on the front page of your local newspaper:

"The News has learned that a textbook banned six weeks ago from the Whitefield school system because of parental objection to its profanity is currently being used in the local school system. The book, *Literature For Today's World* is one of the many language arts texts adopted last spring by this corporation.

"Parents' main objection to the book centers around the use of the words "damn," "hell," "God," "Jesus,"; and also some people have disapproved of the depiction of Biblical stories as myths and legends and to the including of several pictures of classical art portraying nudity. An interview with Larry Hamilton, a teacher who served as chairperson of the textbook adoption committee in the field of language arts this year, confirmed the textbook was on the approved list for this district.

"Hamilton said a committee of teachers from each school evaluates the books that are approved for use each year, but that it is impossible to examine every page and that sometimes oversights can be made. When told the content of the book, Hamilton said he felt that it may not be appropriate for the seventh grade level and indicated a further investigation should be made into the matter. Hamilton pointed out that present-day English teachers are caught in the dilemma of attempting to select textbooks that will set an example to pupils, 'When we try to select a good novel for students, we are hard pressed to find a book that does not have some profanity.'

"Middle School Principal F. William Kendall said, 'There are objections to the profanity in it. I have to really question it when you discipline individuals for swearing and then force them to read a book which contains some of those words. I wonder if we are not setting up a double standard.'

"Charles Whittle, regional director of sales for the textbook firm, has indicated that the complaints are the first the company has received since the second edition has been in use. An earlier edition of the book has been in print for several years; however,

211

Whittle estimated that a few of the stories were changed when the textbook's second edition was published last year.

"The book is one of seven recommended by the State Department of Public Instruction."

### Becoming Involved

1. What was the basic objection to the use of the book?

2. What issues are involved here in regard to school—community relations?

3. What do the comments by the principal and the textbook representative seem to indicate about society?

### Field Exploration

Ask your professor to arrange for a person from the state department of education or the local education office to explain the procedures of textbook adoption. As you listen to the answer, think of how you can avoid problems with parents over future reading materials.

Also, talk with an English teacher concerning the selection of reading materials. How are they selected? How are readings treated which contain profanity?

### Instant Expert

Arthur Holman became an instant educational expert upon his election to the school board. Although plans had been under way for two years to develop a learning resource center in each school, he and his newly-elected associates began to question the concept. Holman convinced several board members that the idea was expensive and unsound. Although sentiment had run high for this new facility, he pursued his determined effort to discredit the project.

One center was started in one of the older schools in the district. The combination of poorer facilities and few guidelines had created some problems, but the school personnel were attempting to be patient in working through the growing pains. Mr. Holman and the director of secondary education made a surprise visit to the school one day and had some critical observations about the merit of the learning resource center in comparison to its cost. They were indifferent to explanations defending the program.

Unexpected visits became common and ultimately the principal was asked to discontinue the learning resources program. Mr. Holman stated that even though the constituents had not expressed many viewpoints the board was convinced that people were not happy with the program and he urged discontinuation of the experiment.

After a meeting with the board, the principal convened the staff to interpret the attitudes of the governing body. Many of the teachers were disturbed. When word of the meeting spread, several feelings began to surface and a real division of opinion developed. The morale of the school seemed to be deteriorating. It appeared that the learning resources center might be discontinued without any type of hearing or evaluation.

### Becoming Involved

1. What was wrong with Mr. Holman's opposing the new facility on the basis that he thought it was expensive and unsound?

2. Since this appears to be a matter between the school board and the administration, how are teacher-community relations affected?

3. How can school personnel respond to a critical board member?

### Field Exploration

If possible arrange for a member of the local school board to come to the class and discuss some of the problems which have arisen and how they have been resolved. Ask how much authority the board exercises.

If this cannot be arranged, attend a meeting of the local board of education (they are open to the public) and note the kinds of decisions which are made.

213

## You Owe Your Soul to the Company Store

Marjorie Wilson was a dedicated teacher. She was an honor student in college and she had kept up with professional developments during her initial teaching years. She was liked by students and considered by her supervisors to be an excellent teacher. All of her evaluations had reflected competence in her position.

Since her teaching record was unblemished, Marjorie had assumed that she would be accepted for tenure without question. As the time for the final decision drew near, she was called into the principal's office for a tenure conference. She was commended as a good teacher, and Mr. Sparks indicated that he would like to have her continue on his staff. Then he made the surprise statement, "I hope that you will consider moving into the school district. The board has adopted the policy that tenured teachers must live in this district."

Marjorie was stunned, "But I only live thirty minutes from the school. We own our home in the community, and it is necessary for my husband's work that we live in Hastings. I have never had any conflict living out of the district, and I think that my teaching record indicates that I have been able to adjust."

"That is not the question at all. We all think that you are a very fine teacher. It is just that the board feels that since the district pays your salary, you should contribute to it by living in the community and supporting its business and social functions. I realize that it is a difficult decision for you, but perhaps you would consider moving just over the district line where your husband will not be too far away from his work and you would technically meet the requirements of the policy.

Marjorie thought about the situation. Positions in her immediate area were scarce and she and her husband really needed the additional income. However, she was reluctant to leave her comfortable home and she was distressed that the board felt that she owed her complete self to the community because the funds for her salary came from that area. She had little time to decide because the board would be meeting in three days and if she did not consent, they would not renew her contract.

214

### *Becoming Involved*

1. What was the stated reason for asking Marjorie to move to the community as a condition for receiving tenure?

2. Can a school board deny tenure in spite of a good teaching record?

3. What alternatives are available for Marjorie if she decides that this condition is unfair?

4. What are the implications of a policy which requires teachers to live in the district where they teach?

5. Should a teacher feel obligated to spend his money in the community where he teaches?

### *Field Exploration*

Ask a few teachers who do not live in the district if they have felt any pressure to move. If so, how have they reacted to the urging?

If you have the opportunity to talk with citizens, try to determine whether they think teachers should reside in the community, and why.

### WHAT THE EXPERTS SAY

The school is a reflection of the community. This proposition seems well accepted, but the problems seem to arise in determining what the community really is and what it wants from its schools. Are the loud complaints the voice of the responsible citizens of the area?

Since the school is considered to be effective in molding students, many citizens scrutinize what is happening and feel that they have to be ever vigilant to the schools' presenting a different moral code than the one considered acceptable by an individual or group. Books seem to be a prime target. An article in *The American School Board Journal*[2] indicates that today in this country book banning is more alive than it has been since the fifties. "Teaching of English in some states has become embarrassingly in-

---

[2]M. Chester Nolte. "Banning Books: An Ancient Sport Makes a Rowdy Comeback Among School Boards," *American School Board Journal* 160, pp. 25-43, May, 1973.

sipid. The curriculum has been arranged so that the students· never will read about drugs, liquor, love, or life." Anyone interested in the subject of banned books will enjoy the article's extensive list of books which have been banned in public schools in this country.

The claim in the above article is supported by a recent Gallup Poll of Public Attitudes Toward Education.[3] When asked how much consideration should be given to parents' views in deciding whether to keep controversial textbooks in schools, 76 percent of the public said that some or a great deal of consideration should be given. It seems apparent that the voices of the parents will be heard in this matter, especially in regard to textbooks for the younger students.

What do teachers teach in the moral realm? Dr. Lawrence Kohlberg[4] recommends that teachers teach the principles of moral judgment and thereby facilitate the moral development of their students without prejudicing the particular values that students will find for themselves. Dr. Kohlberg submits that children progress through three major steps as they mature in their moral thinking:

1. Pre-conventional - instinctive impulses are modified by rewards and punishments.

2. Conventional - behavior is controlled by anticipation of praise or blame.

3. Post-conventional - behavior is regulated by principles embodying generality, consistency, and comprehensiveness.

He feels it is the role of the teachers to help students move to the post-conventional stage by judging statements which have moral implications rather than by the teacher's uncritical sermonizing. This may prove to present some basis for conflict with the community unless it understands the process by which this stage is developed.

[3]George Gallup, "Seventh Annual Gallup Poll of Public Attitudes Toward Education," *Phi Delta Kappan* 57:4, pp. 227-241, December, 1975.

[4]Lawrence Kohlberg, "Moral Education in the Schools: A Developmental View," *School Review* 74:1-30, Spring, 1966.

The American school has been, and in all probability will continue to be embroiled in controversy concerning its role. One of the most vivid examples is the textbook controversy in Kanawa County, West Virginia[5] This struggle continued for months and brought violence to the community. School buses were the targets of shotgun blasts and lives were threatened. It is not infrequent to read that meetings are held which question the role of the schools in regard to religious affairs and in the treatment of controversial subject matter.

Controversies originate in all likelihood from the assumption that the schools are powerful forces in shaping the value codes of the young. Citizens, naturally, try to protect their pupils from school personnel whom they suspect of imposing alien beliefs upon students. Theoretically, teachers are legally prohibited from forcing their dogmas upon students; however, this does not imply that values are to be excluded from the curriculum. As explained by Beauchamp[6], "values are products of our culture . . . And for an important institution like the school not to transmit and generate values is incredible."

Conflict often emerges over what values are to be espoused and content which is to be taught. Community residents often insist that since they support the schools they have total right to determine the curriculum. Educators often feel a responsibility to go beyond the transmitting of already adopted community values and to introduce new views and content to improve the community. An examination of the history of legal contests between schools and other parts of the community gives little hope that such disputes will ever disappear. Perhaps this is not all bad, though, since our way of life is based upon such fundamental premises as the citizen's right to challenge any institution on any matter. Furthermore, it may be significant that the community feels that the schools have an important role in influencing the direction of society.

Many conflicts between school and community result from poor communication. Schools are responsible for establishing and

[5]Franklin Parker, *The Battle of the Books: Kanawha County*, Phi Delta Kappa, Bloomington, IN, 1975.

[6]George A. Beauchamp, *Curriculum Theory*, The Kagg Press, Wilmette, IL, 1975.

217

maintaining an effective system for disseminating information. As a result of poor communications between beginning teachers and parents, many teachers drop out at the end of their first year. Information for involving the community in the orientation of beginning teachers is available;[7] so are guidelines for improving the effectiveness of community councils.[8] [9] [10]

Community involvement is essential for cooperation and uninterrupted education. According to one expert, it is more. It is "one main hope for reform in public schools." [11] Perhaps the implication is that since communities want to participate in the governance of their schools, educators should look for opportunities to engage the community in direct participation in decisions and programs instead of unilaterally making decisions and then attempting to justify them when complaints follow. In effect, the teacher cannot escape the fact that community and schools must work together, and that one will constantly be influencing the other.

## DISCUSSION OF QUESTIONS

### The Rise And Fall of Mr. Dukes

1. *What do you know about Mr. Dukes' students which gives support to his teaching techniques?* Many of his students are college bound; therefore, the fact that he is very demanding and challenging may be well justified.

2. *Why was Mr. Dukes harassed by the community at large?* It seems that Mr. Dukes is resented in some circles because his economic views are oriented toward a value system which is somewhat different from the prevailing community view.

[7]Richard E. Brown, "Community Involvement in Staff Orientation and In-Service," N ASSP *Bulletin* 57:377, December, 1973, pp. 26-30.

[8]Susan Jacoby, "Community Control Can Work," *Learning* 2:51-4, December, 1973.

[9]Dorothy Fagan, "Citizen Advisory Committee," *Thrust for Education Leadership* 3:1, October, 1973, pp. 18-19.

[10]Ann H. Barkelew, "Organizing the School and the District for Public Relations," *Thrust for Education Leadership* 3:1, October, 1973, pp. 20-1.

[11]Don Davies, "The Emerging Third Force in Education," *Inequality In Education,* No. 15, November, 1973, pp. 5-12.

3. *Should a teacher be permitted to select his own preferred teaching style?* As indicated earlier, the teacher should be permitted to choose how he will teach because he is the expert in this area. But what about the selection of content? Should the layman intervene? It is unrealistic to believe that citizens will stand by silently and let teachers teach ideas which are contrary to prevailing community beliefs. It should be remembered that the community built the school to serve it and that one of the major responsibilities of all schools is to prepare the student to move into the surrounding society.

4. *Should the community be permitted to impose its values on Mr. Dukes' way of teaching?* As an agent of society the school must respect the community's values. If it seeks to improve society by introducing change it should do so gradually.

## Open Discussion of a Closed Topic

1. *Can the study of premarital sex in this class be justified?* Possibly. This class was apathetic toward the traditional family-budget unit, and the topic seems logical for a class of this type. The students should be mature enough to deal with the sensitive nature of the subject matter.

2. *What was the real basis for Mrs. Marshall's problem?* Mrs. Marshall's problem emerged from a breakdown in communication. The parents were blaming her for saying something that she did not intend to insinuate.

3. *Suppose that you are a fellow teacher at this school and Mrs. Marshall comes to you for advice. What suggestions can you offer?* Since this problem, like many between teachers and parents, developed from poor communication, Mrs. Marshall should correct the informational error. It is imperative that she remain objective and unemotional.

## It Said, "Damn"

1. *What was the basic objection to the use of the book?* It contained words which the parents found objectionable.

2. *What issues are involved here in regard to school-community relations?* One, of course, is the question of who selects the literature which is to be read. Another concerns whether the schools should present students a broader concept of life; a third issue is whether a double standard is being applied in that the objectionable words appear daily in the media and in conversation.

3. *What do the comments by the principal and the textbook representative seem to indicate about society?* They seem to point out that society in general is more tolerant now than it was a few years ago. The comments may also imply that the role of the school is to help students analyze literature and values instead of merely attempting to impose standards.

## Instant Expert

1. *What was wrong with Mr. Holman's opposing the new facility on the basis that he thought it was expensive and unsound?* He did not seem to possess the type of expertise necessary for judging an operation such as the learning resource center. Therefore, he needed to seek a broader basis for evaluation and maybe involve some people from the community and faculty.

2. *Since this appears to be a matter between the school board and the administration, how are teacher-community relations affected?* The conflict affects the daily operation of the school and obviously makes it more difficult to teach effectively. The question of sovereignty obviously will cause some teacher-community interaction.

3. *How can school personnel respond to a critical board member?* School boards are usually comprised of social leaders in the community who have been successful in their fields. When they are elected to serve on the school board, they may not be aware of their function and their role in this office. The teacher can assist with this problem by offering his knowledge or point of view at meetings of the board of education or through the local teachers association. This is especially needed when members begin forcing those changes upon the schools which conflict with the teacher's area of expertise.

## You Owe Your Soul to the Company Store

1. *What was the stated reason for asking Marjorie to move to the community as a condition for receiving tenure?* The board of education has mandated that all tenured teachers live in the community on the grounds that teachers should support those individuals who pay their salaries.

2. *Can a school board deny tenure in spite of a good teaching record?* Although good teaching is usually the prime consideration, a teacher conventionally serves at the will of the board until tenure is granted. Technically, a non-tenured teacher can be released for no reason.

3. *What alternatives are available for Marjorie if she decides that this condition is unfair?* She may find a friend in her local teachers' association. An appeal to the board could be beneficial since she has a good teaching record and has an established home in an adjacent community. Sometimes pupil support and parental disapproval can be effective in presenting a point of view. However, ethics dictate that any movement of this type should be initiated by someone other than she and that she should not encourage such support.

4. *What are the implications of a policy which requires teachers to live in the district where they teach?* Such a policy can jeopardize the teachers' security in their civil rights. It denies teachers basic freedoms guaranteed to other groups. If carried to extreme, it could lead to complete control of a teacher by one or two members of a community.

5. *Should a teacher feel obligated to spend his money in the community where he teaches?* No. He has rendered service for the stipend which he receives. There should be no strings attached to his salary. The citizen should also be made aware that an entire teacher's salary does not necessarily come from local funds. The state assumes some financial responsibility and many teachers are paid through some type of federal grant. There is no way that a teachers' salary should be required to remain in the school district.

## POST-ASSESSMENT

|  | A G R E E | D I S A G R E E | U N D E C I D E D |
|---|---|---|---|

### How Do You Feel?

1. The relationship of the teacher to the community should be similar to that of an employee to an employer. — — —

2. Ultimately a teacher should obey his own professional conscience rather than submit to community pressure. — — —

3. Controversial reading material should be included in the curriculum if it has value even though there may be parental objection. — — —

4. The school should be a lamp not a mirror; i.e. it should lead the community rather than reflect it. — — —

5. A teacher should comply with the demands of the community only in sensitive curriculum areas like sex education. — — —

### What do you think?

1. The most frequent cause of difficulties between teacher and community relates to curriculum. — — —

2. School officials must learn to interpret the true needs of the community and find ways of fulfilling them. — — —

3. Teachers must satisfy the requests of parents even when their desires seem unreasonable. — — —

4. When the board of trustees uses poor judgment which results in potential damage to the school program, teachers are obligated to react. — — —

5. Community feelings are usually so diverse that there is no way that a teacher can actually be aware of prevailing views. — — —

222

## SELF-ASSESSMENT:

Now that you have completed the post-assessment, compare your pre- and post-assessment scores. Check those questions for which there is disagreement between responses. Examine your reasons for changing your responses. When possible, cite the specific reason which caused your change of opinion.

1. What is the proper role of the community in school governance and curriculum?

2. Should a teacher adhere to community standards?

3. In what ways can a teacher influence a community?

## FURTHER INVOLVEMENT

AMERICAN SCHOOL BOARDS ASSOCIATION, "A Veteran Boardman's Advice: How to Deal with Controversy in Your District," *American School Board Journal* 159:30-32, August, 1972.

Presents two rather significant problems from the point of view of a board member. Indicates one person's idea about how a board should reasonably approach complaints from the public concerning sex education and curriculum innovation. Not all board members are opponents of teachers, as the article demonstrates.

FANTINI, MARIO, *The People and Their Schools: Community Participation*, Phi Delta Kappa, Bloomington, IN, 1975, 37 pp.

Discusses the problems and processes involved in communication. Indicates several types of participation which have featured community involvement.

NATIONAL EDUCATION ASSOCIATION, *Today's Education* 64:4, Nov.-Dec., 1975, pp 68-86.

A special feature explores many aspects of home-school relationships, including a guideline on how to confer with angry parents.

PARKER, FRANKLIN, *The Battle of the Schools: Kanawha County*, Phi Delta Kappa, Bloomington, IN, 1975, 34 pp.

A Case history of the textbook battle in Kanawha County, West Virginia. Attempts to explain why it happened.

PHI DELTA KAPPA, Phi Delta Kappan, September, 1972, Bloomington, IN.

Presents a variety of articles focusing on topics related to community involvement ranging from public attitudes toward education to a discussion of what schools are for. Many aspects of community relationships and involvement are discussed. Includes a Gallup Poll of public opinions of American schools.

STINNETT, T. M., DRUMMOND, WILLIAM H., and GARRY, ALICE W., *Introduction to Teaching*, Charles A. Jones Publishing Co., Worthington, OH, 1975, Chapter 6.

Explains what the community expects of a teacher, reports some indications of the status of teachers, describes how teachers and community are interdependent, and suggests ways teachers might be involved in community affairs.

WILLIAMS, CATHARINE, *The Community as Textbook*, Phi Delta Kappa, Bloomington, IN., 1975, 30 pp.

Indicates how teachers may utlize resources in the community for teaching and learning.

## Chapter Twelve

# THE ECONOMIC SCENE AND THE TEACHER

## PRE-ASSESSMENT

|  | AGREE | DISAGREE | UNDECIDED |
|---|---|---|---|

### How do you feel?

1. Teachers should learn to accept conditions as they are so far as facilities, supplies, and equipment are concerned. — — —

2. If the school fails to provide adequate instructional materials, it is not unreasonable to assess students for the purchase of needed supplies. — — —

3. The economic condition of a school reflects the economic state of the community. — — —

4. Teachers should be involved in making decisions about purchasing books, other materials, and equipment. — — —

5. The economic philosophy of a school is reflected in class size. — — —

### What do you think?

1. The economic retrenchment for most schools is actually less severe than teachers are frequently led to believe. — — —

2. Saving money by cutting back school supplies is an ironic, long-term loss. — — —

3. Teachers should not conform to demands to save money to the extent that they sacrifice quality in learning. — — —

4. A scarcity of equipment and material may actually be an asset since it can stimulate teachers to think, create, design, and invent. — — —

5. The wealthiest school is not necessarily the best school. — — —

## INTRODUCTION

School finance represents a conservative approach to economics. Although critics often refer to a new school building as a palace, closer inspection reveals that it usually has been stripped of the frills and the word has been practicality in design and construction. Funds are carefully appropriated and closely audited to see that there is no excess in the budget. There is a frequent tendency to reduce instructional supplies on the assumption that they may not be needed or that the appropriation may be excessive. School budgets normally do not contain funds for bonuses or for expensive conventions.

When the economy is in a period of inflation or recession, economic retrenchment sometimes occurs. Decreases in budget allotments for schools force administrators to try to stretch every dollar to its limit. Class sizes may be increased in order to reduce instructional costs, and teachers may be asked to save money wherever possible. Schools are forced to assign priorities, and this may mean the reduction or elimination of classes which are expensive to operate. Since it is not possible to have everything wanted or even everything needed, the schools must sacrifice some of the less standard programs like advanced or vocational studies. The really serious problem emerges when the operating allotment is still too small to provide for all the necessities. When this occurs, teachers must often sacrifice materials and equipment which they know will lower the quality of learning in their classes.

Sometimes those who make the allotments are not sensitive to the priorities necessary for optimal educational experiences. It is the teacher's responsibility to communicate the seriousness of the need for specific materials and equipment in his classes. It is also the teacher's duty to see that maximum utilization is made of available supplies.

The following cases depict some of the situations which can result from limited resources. Note the way that teaching practices can be affected. Also, attempt to determine how a teacher should react and try to state a few generalizations which will guide you as a teacher when you are involved in similar situations.

## IN THE CLASSROOM
## Can You Afford the Solution?

Mr. Green's algebra classes were doing great with homework and class participation, but the test results were constantly poor. Although he was an inexperienced teacher, he soon learned that the students were performing well in class because all they had to do to secure answers for the problems was to refer to the back of the book. Then, when the books were unavailable, they were not able to solve the equations.

After giving the matter some thought, Mr. Green inquired to see if new resources could be secured for the class which would prompt more in-depth study. The principal indicated that he could not authorize the expenditure because there were insufficient funds for such purchases. He suggested instead that Mr. Green attempt to discover some creative techniques of teaching so that there would be less reliance upon the problems in the book.

Mr. Green concluded that creative teaching required the accessibility of additional resource material. He located a book which presented problems requiring logical thinking and analysis. Perhaps a class set of these would help him communicate to the class. He did some quick tabulation and concluded that he would ask each student to contribute a total of $1.00 each so that class sets were available.

When he announced the decision, there were some student protests. The complaints gathered momentum, as some parents objected, stating that classroom materials were covered in the text rental budget. Mr. Scott discussed the matter with the teacher again and informed him that school policy precluded the additional purchase of resource materials.

Mr. Green was still left with his initial problem.

### Becoming Involved
1. What was Mr. Green's first attempt to solve the problem?
2. Should students be required to spend money above and beyond the guaranteed cost of a textbook or rental fees?

3. Perhaps Mr. Green's first mistake was his consulting the principal. What do you think?

4. What alternative solutions could be suggested for this problem?

5. What seem to be the economic factors affecting this situation?

### Field Exploration

Talk with a department chairperson, teacher, or administrator concerning textbook policy. Are books purchased or rented? What is the estimated cost for required books for a school year?

Also try to find out if supplementary materials can be secured when the teacher feels that he needs them. Are students ever asked to make any additional purchases?

In the total process, see if you can determine what the economic policy of the school is in regard to the procurement of resources and materials. Why do you think that the operating policy has been accepted?

## Just One More Row

Jo Ellen entered her new classroom and was amazed at the number of chairs that were neatly arranged from the front to the back of the room. She quickly counted the number of seats and realized that her classes could approximate 35 each. Why had an extra row been added since her visit to the school some weeks ago?

The answers were soon provided during the pre-school orientation for new teachers. The principal informed them that the budget had been reviewed and the corporation would not be able to employ as many teachers as originally assumed. She asked that the teachers be understanding in accepting additional class sizes. In most cases, she explained, not more than five or six students had been added to a section.

Jo Ellen was disturbed, not only because her classroom was crowded but also because she planned to do a lot of individualized teaching and require a considerable amount of writ-

228

ing which would be graded. It appeared now that this would be impossible.

### Becoming Involved

1. How did the school officials propose to alleviate the economic situation?

2. How is a teacher affected when class sizes are increased in a move to save money?

### Field Exploration

The next time that you visit a school, count the number of students in several classes. Observe also the teaching techniques used by the teacher. Does there seem to be any relationship between class size and teaching procedure?

## The Company Is On Strike

An economic cloud darkens the picture for Midville School this year. Since this is a one-industry town, the economic condition of the community focuses on the ability of the company to produce jobs. Unfortunately, a strike has closed the plant for three months, so the economic crunch is being felt in many ways in this area.

The school is having to make some adjustments. Many students have not paid their fees, consequently needed revenue for the purchase of equipment and supplies is unavailable. Others have asked to be in school only part-time so they can work to help meet expenses at home. The extracurricular program is at its lowest point ever, since there seems to be neither time nor money for such activity. The central administration has indicated that each department in the school is going to have to reduce its budget twenty percent. There have even been some veiled suggestions that the school corporation will be unable to meet the payroll if the strike continues much longer.

The impact in the classroom is obvious. With a scarcity

229

of resources and a smaller number of students, many adjustments have to be made. The entire mood is tense as pointed remarks between the strike sympathizers and those opposed to it clash in class discussions. Some students simply do not seem to comprehend what is happening and it is difficult to communicate to them what the financial realities actually are.

## Becoming Involved

1. What seems to be the main message of this case study?

2. What kinds of decisions do teachers have to make when they are involved in a situation such as this one?

3. What are some personal concerns that teachers might have in a situation such as this?

## Field Exploration

It is obvious that the educational world does not exist apart from the economic world. As you visit a school, note the kinds of economic influences, both direct and subtle, which have an impact on the school's operation. The class may want to divide responsibility by having some members look at the instructional program, others at the extracurricular program, and others at the physical setting. If you can secure this information from more than one school, you may have some interesting notes to compare.

It might also be worthwhile to determine where the resources are secured to operate the school. Are there any financial giants in the community who contribute a sizeable amount of the funds for the operation of the school? Do they attempt to affect policy in any way? How are teachers affected in this situation?

## Is This For Real?

Ann Block was happy to finally break away from college life and begin teaching. She was so giddy in fact that she applied for and accepted a position by telephone without ever seeing the school.

When Ann made her first visit to the remote rural school, she saw that it was small and dismal appearing. The exterior had been neglected, and there was much loose paper which was swept around the school campus by the wind. Inside, the halls were tall, narrow and dark.

Mr. Duncan, the principal, was a pleasant man, and he seemed delighted to meet Ann. As he escorted her to her classroom, he informed her that initially there would be a somewhat limited amount of instructional materials but she could expect to gradually increase her supplies throughout the year. Ann assured him that she understood the situation and that she would not be unrealistic in her expectations.

When Ann returned home, she realized that she had been so excited about the new position that she failed to inquire about the laboratories, and with three sections of biology and one section of botany, she would spend much, if not most, of her time in the labs. She dismissed the idea when she remembered that some of the rooms were being painted, assuming that the laboratories were probably located there.

On the following Monday, Ann returned to a totally different environment. What seemed to be mobs of students came rushing, talking, and buzzing up and down every corridor. She found her homeroom and within two minutes her professional career had begun as she learned to wrestle with the mundane realities of making out rosters, collecting fees, and assigning books.

It wasn't until noon that she had an opportunity to inquire about the laboratories, only to find that the school had none. She would be doing all of her teaching in her homeroom; yet there were no gas outlets for heat, no running water, and not even a demonstration table. Ann found all of the science equipment available for her classes in the closet at the back of the room--one 1000 ml. beaker, one 500 ml. beaker, a small box of two-holed stoppers, a few feet of rubber tubing, and a mixture of red and blue litmus paper which had faded so that the colors were almost indistinguishable. This just couldn't be for real! But, at this point, what could she do? When she asked Mr. Duncan for materials, he informed her that he had already ordered some equipment for her room, and the science budget was exhausted for the semester. She left school that first day wondering how she could possibly teach in that environment.

### Becoming Involved

1. Is the outside appearance of a school building a good indicator of the financial status of the school?

2. Had the principal really been honest with Ann?

3. During an interview, how far should the applicant question the interviewer about the availability of equipment and materials?

4. Is a principal or department chairperson justified in ordering supplies without consulting the teacher?

### Field Exploration

Talk with an experienced teacher in your subject area, asking what equipment, facilities, and supplies are most important. Take your list to the department chairperson in at least two schools, inquiring which items are available for all of the teachers in his department.

## The Year of the Paper Shortage

Never before had there been so many efforts to economize. Teachers were reminded almost daily to be frugal with all their supplies and materials. Money-saving suggestions were distributed on a regular basis.

Keith Murphy, an irrepressible young professional, was both amused and annoyed by all these directives. He felt that the people who made the decisions were "penny wise and pound foolish," i.e., in the efforts to save money, they were losing the opportunity to get more from their major investment--the teachers. His "money-saving tips" which he regularly posted on the faculty bulletin board delighted the teachers but irritated the administrative personnel. His essay, "The Year of the Paper Shortage," posed a number of amusing incidents that ostensibly occurred because a teacher had to submit a requisition in triplicate for three sheets of paper to use for lesson planning.

The objection was a reaction to policies such as those which restricted the amount of paper and duplication supplies, which curtailed educational field trips, and which virtually eliminated the addition of supplemental books of any kind. The teachers found that they had a classroom and students. They were then admonished to be creative in securing any needed supplies and materials. The situation was uncomfortable, but there apparently was no alternative but to live with an austere budget this year because sufficient money was not appropriated to provide any additional resources.

### Becoming Involved

1. What assumptions seem to be implicit in the school policy?
2. Should a teacher accept economic conditions like the ones depicted in this case study?

### Field Exploration

If you have an opportunity to do any teaching, plan and make a presentation which calls for nothing more than a teacher and pupils. Do not use any instructional materials at all. What were the results? What were the handicaps and benefits?

## The Beginning Salary

Don Buley was at the point of receiving his teaching certificate and securing a position. He had been notified of two promising vacancies and he interviewed with both school systems.

The first community was in an area that appeared to be less wealthy than most in the state. The school was old and obviously not too well-equipped. He studied the salary scale and observed that the beginning salary was $500 higher than the norm quoted by the university placement service. Was this a mistake? He was also reminded by the personnel officer of the school that their school year was two weeks shorter than some of the other schools in the area.

233

The second position was available in a larger city which seemed to display more affluence. The school was more modern and better equipped than the first one. Don obviously was impressed and was ready to accept the position until he noticed that the first-year salary was significantly less than the one offered by the first community. Furthermore, the school year was two weeks longer. When he expressed some surprise, the personnel director called his attention to the total salary schedule and indicated that they placed premium on career teachers and cited the fact that their salary peaked at a figure which was approximately $3,000 per year in excess of other systems.

Don was puzzled. He checked the salary schedule of the first school and discovered that its top stipend was indeed much lower in spite of the good beginning salary. He was interested in both positions and he needed more income at present, but he liked the possibility of career teaching with the promise of more income once he had become an established teacher. Which one should he choose?

## Becoming Involved

1. What are some possible explanations for a school offering an excellent beginning salary but a low career salary?

2. What are some reasons for offering a low beginning salary but providing a higher career salary?

3. What economic beliefs guide each system?

4. Which position should Don accept?

## Field Exploration

See if you can secure the published salary schedules of a few schools (include large as well as small communities). What are the differences between the initial salaries and the top salaries? Select a hypothetical situation where fifty teachers are employed. Place proportionate amounts of teachers in the various experience categories. Now look at two of the more contrasting salary schedules. Which system is paying the most for its teachers? What conclusions can you draw from this analysis? Are there economic advantages to having several young teachers?

## WHAT THE EXPERTS SAY

Do the cases in this chapter reflect singular incidents or do they provide clues about the attitude of the public toward the economics of education? Although the research does not describe the conditions in such isolated incidents, it does provide a broad concept which seems to help explain why such circumstances occur.

Are all schools plagued by insufficient resources? No. There is much economic inequality in the amount of support given to schools. For example, while one school district in Texas spends $5334 per year on each student; another district spends $264.[1] Differences in the amounts of money raised per pupil by two districts (and they may even border each other) and the resulting differences in the quality of education they offer can be quite marked.[2] Wide variations in effort and in ability to support education are a major obstacle to substantial equality of educational opportunity in all states. The great variations may depend upon the wealth of the district, the amount of effort the governmental unit puts forth to support education and the number of pupils served.

There seems to be a high positive correlation between a public school student's socioeconomic status and the amount of money spent on education. School service components correlate positively with pupil performance (student-teacher relations, in-service education of teachers, number of classes taught, supplementary teaching materials, etc.)[3]. It would appear, then, that more money will provide better education for youth.

By some ironic coincidence, the evidence that financial equality is needed for better education has been accompanied by the fact that the needs of the schools have steadily met taxpayer resistance.[4] According to the Americana Encyclopedia 1974 Annual, "taxpayers have expressed their dissatisfaction with costs and other aspects of education by voting against school bond

[1] Kenneth Carlson, "Equalizing Educational Opportunity," *Review of Educational Research*, 42:453-75, Fall, 1972.

[2] Roe L. Johns, Director, *Future Directions for School Financing*, National Education Finance Project, 1212 Southwest Fifth Ave., Gainesville, FL, 1971, p. 59.

[3] Carlson, *op. cit.*

[4] Johns, *op. cit.*, p. 59.

235

issues. Fewer than half of the school board issues recently presented to the nation's voters were approved."[5] Is it any wonder
that so many schools do not have adequate equipment? The National Education Finance Project found that needed vocational
programs are lacking in many schools.[6]

The economic equality theory of education is not accepted by
all parties, though, and there is some research which suggests that
money is not the only answer to securing better results in school.
A study of British schools summarized in the *Education Yearbook*
concluded that once expenditures have risen above a certain
zone, money doesn't seem to matter that much in terms of what
happens to students.[7] In 1971, the Rand Corporation conducted a
review and synthesis of research findings on the effectiveness of
education. They found that . . . in the range of current educational
practice, regarding levels of expenditure and types of teaching
there is nothing that consistently and unambiguously makes a
difference in student outcomes. They concluded that increasing
expenditures on traditional educational practices is not likely to
improve educational outcomes substantially and that there seem
to be opportunities for significant redirections . . . in educational
expenses without deterioration in educational outcomes.[8]

Are the two points of view in complete contrast with each
other? Not necessarily. Donald R. Winkler[9] summarized the
research in the areas of finance and school effectiveness and concluded that dollars *can* make a difference, but the effectiveness of
the dollars spent depends on what resources are purchased with
that money and the characteristics of the students receiving those
resources. Dollars used to employ high quality teachers or money
used to integrate schools by social class may influence student
achievement. In other words, funds can make a difference if spent
on those school inputs which influence student achievement.

[5]*The American*, 1974 Annual, Grolier, Inc., p. 220.

[6]Johns, *op. cit.*, p. 25.

[7]Daniel Moynihan, "Equalizing Education: In Whose Benefit?" *Education Yearbook*, 1973-74, Macmillan Educational Corporation, pp. 139-149.

[8]Harvey Averach, et al., *How Effective is Schooling: A Critical Review and Synthesis of Research Findings*, The Rand Corporation, Santa Monica, CA, pp. 12-13.

[9]Donald R. Winkler, "*Do Dollars for Higher Quality Teachers Make a
Difference?*" *Compact* 6:6, December, 1972, January, 1973, Educational Commission of the States, 300 Lincoln Tower, 1860 Lincoln St., Denver, pp. 13-16.

In summary, it may be observed that the lack of supplies and equipment may reflect economic retrenchment and inequality of commitment which suggests that teachers and the public should give more attention to financial priorities. It seems, finally, that the caliber of the teacher seems to have an effect regardless of the economic condition of the school, but that the better equipped schools seem to generally have the better teachers.

## DISCUSSION OF QUESTIONS

### Can You Afford The Solution?

1. *What was Mr. Green's first attempt to solve the problem?* He wanted to purchase new books but his request was denied.

2. *Should students be required to spend money above and beyond the guaranteed cost of a textbook or rental fees?* Since students are the ones who would likely benefit from better materials, the appeal seems reasonable. However, a teacher should not abuse the privilege, because several requisitions could total up to a substantial expenditure.

3. *Perhaps Mr. Green's first mistake was his consulting the principal. What do you think?* The principal holds the responsibility for the school's expenditure of funds. Therefore, he should be consulted on financial matters, unless it has been delegated to an assistant or a department chairperson.

4. *What alternative solutions could be suggested for this problem?* Mr. Green could have presented similar problems so that the students would not have answers available. He could also have discussed the situation with the class and asked them to help find a solution.

5. *What seem to be the economic factors affecting this situation?* The parsimony of the community and the policy which the school has adopted concerning expenditures seem to be obvious. Another economic-related factor would be whether the expenditure will help students to learn. Good teaching is not necessarily synonymous with increased spending.

237

## Just One More Row

*1. How did the school officials propose to alleviate the economic situation?* They increased class sizes in order to keep from employing additional teachers.

*2. How is a teacher affected when class sizes are increased in a move to save money?* Her work load is increased without additional compensation and her options in selecting teaching techniques may be severely modified.

## The Company Is On Strike

*1. What seems to be the main message of this case study?* The inference seems to be that community economics, especially if it is dominated by one segment, has tremendous effect upon the program of the school.

*2. What kinds of decisions do teachers have to make when they are involved in a situation such as this one?* They have to learn to operate with fewer materials and resources and to be able to justify their expenses more completely. Teachers may have to be more flexible in their instructional styles in order to compensate for the changes in students and the changes in the economic picture. Finally, they likely will find that the curriculum will be affected by the strike, i.e., they will have to recognize that this fact will influence much of what happens in the classroom.

*3. What are some personal concerns that teachers might have in a situation such as this?* Since there is less money, they may be asked to accept responsibilities which normally accord supplementary compensation. They may also have to resist the temptation to get involved because of strong feelings for one side or the other.

## Is This For Real?

*1. Is the outside appearance of a school building a good indicator of the financial status of the school?* Often it is; yet, this does not account for priorities. A school may spend all of its

238

money on obtaining and maintaining a beautiful physical facility and have little left for purchasing equipment. At the other extreme, a large amount may be spent for purchasing equipment at the expense of ignoring the building. The only way to properly assess the availability of equipment and supplies of a school is to visit the school and the teachers in the department in which you would teach.

2. *Had the principal really been honest with Ann?* Yes. He informed her of the limited supply of materials in her department.

3. *During an interview, how far should the applicant question the interviewer about the availability of equipment and materials?* A candidate should feel free to ask any and all questions necessary to ascertain whether he would have access to the materials necessary to do a good job in his teaching.

4. *Is a principal or department chairperson justified in ordering supplies without consulting the teachers?* Although this practice is not uncommon, it is not a wise one, since every dollar should be used to its maximum potential and the teacher should know which items are needed most

## The Year of the Paper Shortage

1. *What assumptions seem to be implicit in the school policy?* It apparently is assumed that a teacher can effectively teach without the benefit of duplicated materials or other resources. The policy also seems to present the premise that there is no other method to secure needed funds. A look at the total budget would also likely reveal that someone thinks that certain other activities are more important.

2. *Should a teacher accept economic conditions like the ones depicted in this case study?* A teacher has an ethical obligation to serve students in the best way that he can. If he feels limited by the lack of materials and supplies, he should make it known. Although protests such as the one in this case are amusing and sometimes successful, a well-considered, documented request will more likely succeed.

239

## The Beginning Salary

1. *What are some possible explanations for a school offering an excellent beginning salary but a low career salary?* It appears that the system wants to be competitive in securing beginning teachers. It may indicate that they plan to employ teachers for only a few years and then assume that they will move to another system. Another possibility is that the system resists tenure and wants to discourage teachers from planning to teach in that system permanently.

2. *What are some reasons for offering a low beginning salary but providing a higher career salary?* The low beginning salary may be an indication that the system has no difficulty in securing the number of beginning teachers that it wishes. The higher peak salary may indicate that they value permanence in the staff and want teachers who will remain in the system.

3. *What economic beliefs guide each system?* Obviously economy is a factor, although each may interpret the word differently. The school offering the higher beginning salary may find that it is more economical to have several good teachers with little experience than it is to have to pay more experienced teachers higher salaries. The second system may feel that it is more economical to retain a staff than to have more replacements.

4. *Which position should Don accept?* This is a real value question involving considerations concerning immediate need for income and career objectives. Most educators would probably opt for the latter school.

| | | | |
|---|:-:|:-:|:-:|
| **POST-ASSESSMENT** | A<br>G<br>R<br>E<br>E | D<br>I<br>S<br>A<br>G<br>R<br>E<br>E | U<br>N<br>D<br>E<br>C<br>I<br>D<br>E<br>D |

### How do you feel?

1. Teachers should learn to accept conditions as they are so far as facilities, supplies, and equipment are concerned. — — —

2. If the school fails to provide adequate instructional materials, it is not unreasonable to assess students for the purchase of needed supplies. — — —

3. The economic condition of a school reflects the economic state of the community. — — —

4. Teachers should be involved in making decisions about purchasing books, other materials, and equipment. — — —

5. The economic philosophy of a school is reflected in class size. — — —

### What do you think?

1. The economic retrenchment for most schools is actually less severe than teachers are frequently led to believe. — — —

2. Saving money by cutting back school supplies is an ironic, long-term loss. — — —

3. Teachers should not conform to demands to save money to the extent that they sacrifice quality in learning. — — —

4. A scarcity of equipment and material may actually be an asset since it can stimulate teachers to think, create, design, and invent. — — —

5. The wealthiest school is not necessarily the best school. — — —

241

## SELF-ASSESSMENT

Now that you have completed the post-assessment, compare it with your pre-assessment scores. Check those items where there is disagreement between responses. Examine your reasons for changing your responses. When possible, cite the specific factors that had some influence on that change.

1. Do you think that the economic situation for the schools will become worse before it gets better?

2. What kinds of adjustments should teachers make to live with economic conditions that are unfavorable?

3. Does the teacher have a responsibility to assist in saving the school money whenever he can without affecting the quality of his teaching?

4. Should a teacher accept a condition which will diminish the quality of educational experiences in his classes?

5. How can a teacher protect materials and equipment in his classrooms?

## FURTHER INVOLVEMENT

HELLER, WALTER W., "The National Economic Setting for Education," *Today's Education* 63:7, Dec., 1973, pp. 66-7, 69-70.

The author provides a brief of the national economic setting for education.

NEILL, G. W. "When Inflation Hits the Schools; the Word is Retrenchment," *Compact* 7:3-6, November, 1973.

When inflation hits, swift economy measures seem to be the immediate answer to the school's problem. The areas most likely affected by cutbacks are school lunches, pupil personnel services, driver education, innovative programs, education for the handicapped, and construction plans.

PHI DELTA KAPPA COMMISSION ON ALTERNATIVE DESIGN FOR FUNDING EDUCATION, "Viable Alternatives for Public School Finance," *Education Digest* 39:2-5, January, 1974.

This article looks at the problem of financing local schools and discusses five alternative possibilities, ranging from local support alone to full state funding. The implications of various funding systems can help to understand why schools are confronted with some of the financial problems that exist.

NATIONAL EDUCATION ASSOCIATION, "School Finance; Symposium," *Today's Education* 62:66-7, November, 1973.

Several scholars, including Walter Heller, present their views on the topic of school finance. The symposium covers such topics as the national economic setting for education and school finance reform. Take a look at the graphs picturing the inequities in various states and districts. It can be an eye-opener.

# INDEX